Peak Performance,
Enjoyment, and Well-Being

=====================================

**Enrich Your Life
Achieve Your Objectives
Elevate Mind-Brain-Body Function
to Its Highest Potential**

=====================================

**Powerful Self-Help Techniques:
Breathing – Movement – Relaxation -
Revitalization – Goal-Setting Visualization**

=====================================

Vortex Energy Therapy

A program developed by

Allan Warrener

BALBOA.
PRESS
A DIVISION OF HAY HOUSE

Balboa Press books may be ordered through
booksellers or by contacting:

Balboa Press
A Division of Hay House
1663 Liberty Drive
Bloomington, IN 47403
www.balboapress.com.au
1 (877) 407-4847

Because of the dynamic nature of the Internet, any web
addresses or links contained in this book may have changed
since publication and may no longer be valid. The views
expressed in this work are solely those of the author and do
not necessarily reflect the views of the publisher, and the
publisher hereby disclaims any responsibility for them.

The author of this book does not dispense medical advice or prescribe
the use of any technique as a form of treatment for physical,
emotional, or medical problems without the advice of a physician,
either directly or indirectly. The intent of the author is only to offer
information of a general nature to help you in your quest for emotional
and spiritual well-being. In the event you use any of the information
in this book for yourself, which is your constitutional right, the
author and the publisher assume no responsibility for your actions.

Any people depicted in stock imagery provided by Thinkstock are
models, and such images are being used for illustrative purposes only.
Certain stock imagery © Thinkstock.

Print information available on the last page.

ISBN: 978-1-4525-3054-3 (sc)
ISBN: 978-1-4525-3055-0 (e)

Balboa Press rev. date: 08/31/2015

Table of Contents

This book is dedicated to my dear wife, Valerie, with love, gratitude, and appreciation for the wonderful life we shared. I now realize that our life together was our destiny, our purpose in life. We were married for more than sixty years (since October 4, 1952) and were blessed with a wonderful family.

Valerie was called to Higher Service in God's Celestial Garden on March 26, 2013. I cherish the beautiful memories and feelings we shared. She was a true friend. I feel blessed that Valerie was my wife.

We embraced and enjoyed being with our family—Paul, Tess, Louise, Peter, and Tim—and were involved in swimming lessons, football, soccer, hockey, and running, in addition to school and church activities and becoming friends with many fine people in our community.

We had many dear friends from all walks of life. We shared the same feelings about people and life in general. There was much purpose in wanting to help people who came to our clinic with a variety of ailments and injuries. Studying Italian enriched our lives, becoming a joy for us to be able to communicate with and help elderly Italian migrants. We very much enjoyed the warm bonds of friendship we all shared.

Valerie told me to finish writing this book. Sharing these wonderful discoveries with which we have been enlightened still remains as our purpose in life. Staunch friends and writing have helped to sustain me along the way.

The book is a summary and the culmination of an ongoing research program spanning more than thirty-seven years. There have been many exciting and amazing discoveries that I would like to share. Through the years, these discoveries have gradually developed into a step-by-step procedure. This therapeutic system and program is known as Vortex Energy Therapy (VET).

The program is a powerful new approach to enjoy better health and well-being. It teaches how to balance and revitalize the body by using self-help techniques with breathing, movement, coordination, relaxation, revitalization, personal development, and goal-setting visualization.

Allan

Introducing Allan Warrener and Vortex Energy Therapy

I have known Dr Allan Warrener for many years as a friend, a fellow Rotarian, and a chiropractor. Allan commenced his career with the Education Department first as a student teacher and then later transferred to the administration side in the Public Service. He later studied and became qualified in supply management. He was employed in large manufacturing organizations and was involved in all facets of supply management, including scheduling, storage, and purchasing.

Valerie and Allan later established two businesses, one involving prams, strollers, and nursery products; the other with all types of blinds, curtains, and drapes, also manufacturing canvas products.

After graduating as a chiropractor as a mature age student, he established a clinic. Val eventually became involved in assisting at the clinic.

Here is a brief summary of some aspects of Allan's life that have taken him in many directions with research and resulted in many amazing discoveries to gradually develop and culminate into this unique, eclectic self-help program—Vortex Energy Therapy (VET).

Allan competed in many sports, but the sport that he enjoyed most of all was running. He recalled that in his early teenage years he became absorbed in studying the different styles of champion sprinters because he was always seeking ways to improve his speed as a sprinter. The main points that he observed with champions was the ease and relaxation with movement, the straight body alignment, high knee lift, balance and coordination, and the pelvic tilt.

At that time, he injured his knee when competing in the broad jump at the intercollegiate sports meeting. He was so impressed with the treatment he received at that time that he thought that he would like to study and become qualified in this neurological and musculoskeletal field, which he eventually did as a mature age student. It would seem that this period was really the beginning of a journey with the objectives that he later set, when he asked himself this question: How can we bring the body to function with maximal efficiency and become capable of performing at one's potential?

He competed in all the classic running events around Victoria—the Stawell Gift, Bendigo Thousand, the Ararat, Maryborough, and Wangaratta Gift meetings. He is an accredited track and field coach and has coached athletes at different periods.

Allan commenced this research program while assisting athletes and sports people by treating their injuries as well as using a variety of methods to improve balance, coordination and strength to complement their training routines and help with improving their performances.

There were three major turning points in Allan's life. The first was studying chiropractic as a mature age student. It was with Val's encouragement and blessing that he took this step, because Val said that she thought that it was his niche in life. The next step was when he commenced this research program. Allan said that the other major turning point in his life was being invited to join the Rotary Club of Footscray and to be able to be involved in playing a part in many wonderful humanitarian projects with Rotary, helping people both locally and internationally. Allan was Club President, 1999–2000. He was honoured to be named a Paul Harris Fellow by The Rotary Foundation of Rotary International in the year 2000 and to receive further recognition with a Paul Harris Fellow (Sapphire) in 2008.

He has always been an innovator and willing to study to improve his education and knowledge in bringing the latest technology to others. Through the years as a chiropractor, he was involved in research with Dr Victor Frank, who developed the therapeutic system Total Body Modification with other colleagues in Australia and overseas. As a result of this research and workshops, Allan received recognition by Dr Victor Frank and his Total Body Modification group as an environmental stress management consultant and for his contributions with research.

He has treated a variety of sporting injuries and ailments in his clinic and studied and researched many systems from around the world regarding health and healing. In this book, he has correlated and merged the ancient knowledge of the East with Western science—that is, with the neurological and musculoskeletal aspects of the body.

For many years, Allan has given presentations and demonstrations and conducted workshops to explain and teach Vortex Energy Therapy to various groups— such as Rotary Clubs, yoga schools and courses, track and field coaches, athletes, naturopaths, and a massage school - people who are interested in Vortex Energy Therapy and enjoying better health and well-being. With the use of each technique, everyone is able to see the immediate improvement and changes that occur each time. With each technique, the criteria for scientific validation of predictability, measurability, and repeatability can be demonstrated.

Allan has always been interested in helping young athletes improve their performances. In recent years, he has very much enjoyed being involved with the Ethiopian community, assisting the soccer players and athletes and being interested in their capabilities and potential. Our Rotary Club of Footscray assisted the Ethiopian community in organizing their annual soccer tournament with clubs from around Australia.

Today we are witnessing a great transition in medical thinking. New methods and treatment are now changing the lifestyles of many. The text offers the reader the opportunity to use these powerful self-help techniques in bringing the body to function at its highest level of efficiency.

H. David Graham, OAM

Allan Warrener: The Man behind Our Rotary Badge

After graduating in 1977 and commencing his chiropractic practice in Footscray, Allan Warrener began a research program while assisting athletes in treating their injuries and using methods to improve balance, coordination, and increase overall strength to improve performances.

Besides treating their injuries, Allan's main objective was to determine how we can bring the body to function with maximal efficiency to assist athletes in performing at their potential. This objective has guided him through the years, culminating in the development of this exciting Vortex Energy Therapy program, with simple self-help techniques for everyone.

As a long-serving member of the Rotary Club of Footscray for over thirty years, Allan was invited to make a presentation at a Rotary meeting and demonstrate some of his theories. With our fit, athletic soccer-playing member Robert on the treatment table, Allan demonstrated a series of techniques to make any necessary corrections, explaining how the different types of stress adversely affect the body, the effects of extreme changes in weather, how the body can be affected with variety of movements, and much more. We were entertained with the agility and soccer skills demonstrated by Robert. With muscle testing, the improvement that occurred with each technique became obvious. There were many witty interjections throughout, and we did have fun!! Allan certainly brought the wow factor to our meeting.

Allan's book describes a therapeutic system that is the culmination of an ongoing research program spanning more than thirty-seven years of testing and including thousands of cases. Many important discoveries have resulted while searching for solutions to help people with a variety of ailments and injuries. Vortex Energy Therapy is a new concept covering many aspects of mind-body function. Although the techniques have been proven numerous times to produce beneficial results with a variety of lesions and ailments and can be used by practitioners for this purpose, the system has now been converted into a complete program that includes powerful self-help techniques that are suitable for everyone. Its objective is for better performance, health, and well-being. I congratulate Allan on the culmination of his work in this excellent publication.

Carol Castano
Rotary Club of Footscray,
Club President 2009–2010

Introduction

I would like to express my sincere thanks to my many dear friends for their kindness and help with the writing of this book. My good friend and chiropractic colleague Lloyd Nelson was instrumental in enrolling me in the course at The Chiropractic College of Australasia. Another good friend, Mahinder Lall, my lecturer in pharmacology and pathology, highly respected within the profession, became excited after reading my earlier notes about the program. Initially I was hesitant in presenting my concepts to such a knowledgeable man. His response was completely unexpected and really surprised me. His words to me: "This is unique! It's eclectic! It's got everything!" His enthusiastic support reinforced my faith, strength, and determination to develop and share our Vortex Energy Therapy program.

Vortex Energy Therapy (VET) is a therapeutic system and program that is suitable for everyone. Its objective is to bring mind-brain-body function to its highest level of efficiency, to enable anyone to enjoy better health and well-being, and to become capable of performing at one's potential. The focus of this program is to teach simple yet powerful self-help techniques such as breathing, movement, relaxation, revitalization, and goal-setting visualization. The program, which is the culmination of thirty-seven years of research, has been well tested and proven in achieving these objectives.

With every step along the way, ever present has been the thought that with the development of each technique, it was important to understand what was happening each time and also to fulfil the scientific validation criteria of predictability, measurability, and repeatability. With each technique, what will happen can be precisely predicted, the immediate improvement after the use of each technique can be measured in different ways, and the same results can be repeated by anyone.

It is pleasing for me to be able to share many exciting and amazing discoveries that you will enjoy and find most beneficial. This book is presented to gladly share the knowledge of numerous groundbreaking discoveries with health practitioners and the many allied groups and organizations concerned about health and well-being. This information could also be of much interest to researchers involved in different fields of health and performance, anyone who might be interested in teaching these VET self-help techniques, and everyone who is interested in improving performance and enjoying better health and well-being with self-help techniques.

The structure of the whole system presents us with a vast configuration. It links the physical and the non-physical aspects, giving us a much broader perception of mind-brain-body function and an extensive structure with seemingly unlimited possibilities for new discoveries and developments in the many various fields of research.

The beginning of this research program

What are the factors affecting performance, health, and well-being? How can we bring the mind-brain-body function to its highest level of efficiency so that anyone is capable of performing at his or her potential? With injuries, imbalances, ailments, or illnesses, are we correcting and eliminating the causes? If not, the body remains predisposed to recurrences. These were some of the questions that have guided me since commencing this research program in 1978.

Providence seems to have replied to my questions and gradually guided me in a step-by-step procedure, in many directions, to study many therapeutic systems and modalities from around the world. Through the years, there have been many exciting discoveries that eventuated as a result of searching for solutions for a variety of injuries, ailments, and a multitude of problems affecting patients who came to our clinic. With the development of all these amazing discoveries and new knowledge, it was realized that this research had gradually culminated into this unique, eclectic system and program: Vortex Energy Therapy.

Assessment of the overall condition of the body

It can be demonstrated how both at a conscious and subconscious level, the mind-brain-body functions as a marvellous biological computer and information about the overall condition of the body can be assessed. With this research program, through years of testing, here is my perception of mind-brain-body function.

One's life force energy, electromagnetic in nature, multidimensional in that it functions at many levels or frequencies in the body, comes from the earth and the universe. It is stepped down through a series of vortexes that function as transformers to refine the earth and universal energies to different levels or frequencies suitable for mind-brain-body function; otherwise, it would be too powerful for the body. The whole body can be envisaged as a vast network of an electromagnetic life force energy circuitry with a series of vortexes both within and surrounding the body, acting as transformers and vital energy centres.

The whole body's surface can be visualized as a touch computer screen with several points on its surface through which information can be accessed and assessed as to the body's overall condition.

All these claims can be demonstrated and confirmed with muscle testing.

Muscle testing has been used in combination with other neurological, musculoskeletal testing as an aid to diagnosis. Muscle testing in this manner is an art that needs to be taught correctly. All of this information regarding mind-brain-body functioning as a biological computer, the body's surface serving as a computer screen, and how to access and assess information with muscle testing is explained in chapter 4.

It was only after retiring as a chiropractor that I had the opportunity to fully develop this VET program. During my years in clinical practice, patients came to our clinic with a variety of injuries and ailments, many of them in severe pain and extremely restricted with their movements.

It was not uncommon to see a person locked into an antalgic posture, which is when a person is locked into a position because of muscle spasm and leans to one side or the other or forward. The muscles go into spasm to protect the body, to some degree, from pain. There would often be patients with severe torticollis, unable to move their necks because of the pain and muscle spasm.

With treatment, many factors needed to be taken into consideration. Whilst some patients might immediately respond favourably to treatment, there could perhaps be many complexities with others. This could be due to varying degrees of degenerative changes in their spines as well as traumas that had occurred during their lives. Each case needed to be assessed individually. Apart from structural lesions, a wide variety of ailments required diagnosis and treatment.

Patients would often ask what caused the severe lower back pain when perhaps all they had done was to bend over to pick something up or some other simple action. At that time, I would usually explain that it would seem that the body was already predisposed to injury because of the overall muscular imbalances and that the strong muscles on one side of the body would pull the whole body out of alignment. We would then discuss ways that could prevent the situation from occurring again. But these were the questions that kept me on track and asking myself how we can bring the body to function with maximal efficiency and help anyone become capable of performing at one's potential.

For the benefit of everyone, it should be explained that chiropractic is concerned with the neurological and musculoskeletal integrity of the body. Chiropractors manually adjust the bones of the body, especially the vertebrae of the spine, to balance the alignment of the whole muscular and skeletal structure. Misalignments of vertebrae along the spine often cause painful nerve root pressure. It has been well acknowledged that chiropractors are highly skilled and qualified in diagnosis and with adjusting the vertebrae in aligning the spine to restore function and often relieving pain caused by nerve root pressure.

Although chiropractic adjustments formed the basis of treatment through my years in clinical practice with very pleasing results, this VET program uses a completely different approach by using powerful, self-help techniques to balance the neurological, musculoskeletal aspects of the body.

It does not involve manual physical adjustments to correct overall structural misalignments, nor does it specifically treat any regions of the body. It is the overall balancing in bringing mind-brain-body function to its highest level of efficiency, with balanced and structural alignment, coordinated movement sequence patterns, and bodily systems functioning in synchronization, having aims of better performance, health, well-being, and becoming capable of performing at one's potential. The VET techniques also correct and eliminate the cause as well as any detrimental factors that are adversely affecting the body. Having retired as a chiropractor, I no longer treat anyone with chiropractic treatment, nor is it the aim of this Vortex Energy Therapy program to specifically treat any condition; again, it is to bring mind-brain-body function to its highest level of efficiency.

Identifying the cause

With testing through the years, it seems apparent that most detrimental factors commence during our early formative childhood years, especially from the period of crawling to the upright posture, becoming balanced and walking. This is the time when muscular imbalances with posture and movement begin to develop and lead to faulty habits. The self-image that is the perception of one's abilities, appearances, and capabilities also begins to develop.

As well as enjoying good health, well-being, and being capable of performing at your potential, the purpose of the program is to assist with self-development in achieving your objectives by using self-help techniques, breathing, movement, relaxation, revitalization, and goal-setting visualization.

The main aim of this program is to balance posture and to coordinate and synchronize the overall musculature of the body with movement. The main principle of Vortex Energy Therapy to be remembered is that the mind-brain-body is comprised of a series of systems designed to function in harmony and synchronization as integral parts of a whole unit.

Feelings are an integral part of mind-brain-body function. Affirmations become powerful when the feelings that the body needs are included. These main feelings are love, gratitude, comfort, security, control, and pleasurable sensual feelings through touch, taste, sound, sight, and smell. Then there is the expression and fulfilment of these feelings.

Chapter 1 includes an affirmation verse in which all of these innate feelings have been interwoven. Reciting this verse will produce immediate and overall beneficial effects in your body because it produces these feelings.

The States of Mind section is a most important part of the whole program because of the influence of the mind on brain-body function. The whole of this section has been classified into four categories, the purpose of which is to develop awareness and recognition of common negative thoughts, attitudes, feelings and emotions, obstacles to learning, communication, and development. Another state of mind example is a mind that is confined within the parameters of reasoning and rational thinking, not listening to and heeding one's thoughts, which give the answers to the knowledge that we are seeking. Then moving to a higher state of mind, there is calmness of mind and becoming open-minded in order to open the doorways to innovation and creativity.

Stress is a major factor adversely affecting the body, predisposing it to injuries and illnesses. Stress can be physical, mental, emotional, or environmental. It is the body's allergic reaction to different environments. The Vortex Energy Therapy program demonstrates techniques to correct and eliminate the detrimental effects of stress and ensures that the body remains stress-free.

The self-image is described as the perception that one has of one's abilities, appearance, and personality. When initially testing anyone, it is most common to be able to demonstrate the adverse influence of self-image on the body. The self-image is submerged in the mind at a subconscious level. There can also be a conscious perception. It will retard or hinder an individual from performing beyond the restricting limitations of this self-image, even though consciously there is a strong desire and wanting to achieve some particular goals. It can be demonstrated how a negative self-image affects the neurological and muscular aspects of mind-body function, which in turn can influence other aspects of function. Developing a new vibrant self-image is discussed in chapter 11.

The mind-brain-body level—the body's control centre

Discovering the mind-brain-body level and how to access this level and make overall corrections is of paramount importance because at this level, we are able to switch into further levels that are connected to every part of the body. And then information can be accessed through the sacrum and coccyx bones about the whole vertebral column and spinal cord.

Partial impairment of the sacral and coccygeal nerves

In chapter 4, which explains mind-brain-body functioning as a marvellous biological computer, there is also much discussed about injury to the spine, spinal cord, sacrum, and coccyx bones. These are ground-breaking discoveries.

It is important to first consult your doctor before commencing any breathing or other techniques.

I would like to emphasize that in explaining about the VET breathing techniques, it is not intended as a criticism of any other form of breathing exercises. During my life, I have always studied and practised relaxation and other forms of breathing exercises, and I have experienced many beneficial results in restoring my health and well-being. I would strongly recommend that you continue with any breathing program that has been advised by your doctor or physiotherapist as being suitable for you.

The Vortex Energy Therapy method is a very relaxed, gentle form of breathing in response to the body's overall requirements. It is the movement along the spine with arching of the lower back and then the lifting and rolling of the shoulders backwards, causing lung capacity to expand, with the result that the air flows automatically and effortlessly in and out through the nostrils.

Chapter 1

Vortex Energy Therapy

A Therapeutic Program
Developed by Allan Warrener

Vortex Energy Therapy (VET) is a powerful new approach for you to enjoy good health and well-being and balance and revitalise your body with breathing, movement, relaxation, personal development, goal-setting, and visualisation self-help techniques.

The program focuses on demonstrating and teaching a variety of self-help techniques, especially those that utilise breathing, movement, and rhythmical arm-swinging exercises. Through the use of simple yet powerful breathing techniques, you can immediately correct and eliminate common detrimental factors and faulty habits, increase overall strength, and align and balance the whole muscular and skeletal structure of the body. Isn't it exciting to know that with just one breath, you can correct and eliminate all these common detrimental factors and faulty habits?

The rhythmical arm-swinging exercise technique ensures that the body is relaxed, balanced, and coordinated, with all muscles functioning in synchronisation whilst walking. It conserves your energy. Having seen this improvement happen countless times, I am confident you will enjoy this program and find it worthwhile.

This program is ideal for people of all ages and can be easily incorporated into your everyday activities. You'll find that this technique enhances your performance in whatever direction your interests might be.

How does the program assist and enhance such a wide variety of sports and activities? It achieves immediate improvement by balancing and coordinating the neurological and musculoskeletal aspects of mind-brain-body functions and ensures synchronisation of the overall body function with movement. Furthermore— and this is a most exciting aspect of the program—the techniques activate the neural pathways to facilitate the movements that are specific to each sport or activity.

Vortex Energy Therapy merges the ancient knowledge of the East with neurological, musculoskeletal, and anatomical aspects of the body. A therapeutic system and a unique, eclectic program, VET embraces knowledge from countries around the world, including China, India, Japan, and Thailand. The integration of all this knowledge and research resulted in the discovery of a new concept. VET has been correlated and tested in parallel with the neurological and musculoskeletal aspects of mind-brain-body function to fulfil the criteria of predictability, measurability, and repeatability required to be deemed scientifically valid.

With each technique, results can be precisely predicted and explained, and the improvement that occurs can be measured in different ways. The same procedure can be repeated by anyone.

When I began to develop this program, my thoughts were focused and productive. *What are the factors that affect performance? How can we bring the body to function at its highest level of efficiency?* If the body is balanced, coordinated, and functioning with maximum efficiency, there is less likelihood that injuries will occur. *In treating injuries, are we also correcting and removing the cause?* Fortunately, it was these thoughts that set the objectives and direction to gradually develop this knowledge in a step-by-step procedure to culminate in Vortex Energy Therapy, a whole therapeutic program.

Although chiropractic therapy has formed the basis of treatment through my years in clinical practice (and with pleasing results), this VET program uses a completely different approach. It does not involve manual or physical adjustments to correct overall structural misalignments. Rather, it is through overall balancing of the musculature that a balanced, structural alignment occurs. VET techniques also correct and eliminate the cause.

The objectives of Vortex Energy Therapy are to teach,

- How to bring mind-body function to its highest level of efficiency,
- How to become capable of performing at one's potential; and
- How to correct and eliminate common detrimental factors and faulty habits.

Developing the Vortex Energy Therapy program to achieve objectives

Many exciting and wonderful discoveries have resulted in the search for solutions to help patients with a variety of ailments and injuries. I realised that all of these new concepts had gradually developed into a complete system and program. Everyone appreciated the immediate and overall beneficial improvement that the VET techniques produced. Patients would ask me, "What do you call this? Is it kinesiology?" No, it's not kinesiology.

Later in the book, I will explain my reasons for naming this program Vortex Energy Therapy. In short, this was so it would not be confused with any other system, practice, or modality.

Assessing the changes and development with testing in this research program

As a chiropractor, my focus with treatment was directed towards the neurological and musculoskeletal aspects of function to ensure overall balance of the body.

Standard orthopaedic muscle testing has presented us with an overall assessment of the condition of the body's musculature and its weaknesses, strengths, and imbalances.

Neurological tests provide further information of dysfunctional muscles, nerve impairment, and gait mechanism, as well as coordination and synchronisation of muscle function with various movement sequences.

Pain is also another way of assessing difference with muscle testing against resistance, with palpation of a muscle or pain at a joint with movement. Equally, there's the relief from pain after using a particular technique.

Improvement with overall muscle strength is measured on a scale of one to ten, ten being a person's current potential strength. Those patients who present with readings between one and four are known to enjoy increases in the seven-to-ten range.

Dr George Goodheart, a chiropractor, discovered that muscle testing, when used in combination with other neurological and musculoskeletal orthopaedic tests, could be used as an aid to diagnosis. (This theory and how it differs from orthopaedic muscle testing will be described later.) It is commonly used by practitioners worldwide as an aid to diagnosis and in locating dysfunctional regions in the body. For this purpose, muscle testing is an art form that needs to be studied. As an aid to diagnosis in combination and in parallel with other tests, it enables the practitioner or researcher to access and assess unlimited information about the body.

Common detrimental factors

With testing through the years, I have found that there are common detrimental factors, many of which can result in a person not feeling well and lacking in energy. Because of muscular imbalances and structural misalignments, these adverse factors predispose the body to injuries and illnesses and also serve as a hindrance to performing at one's potential. Most of these adverse factors are present when initially testing patients. Self-help VET techniques described in later chapters can immediately correct and eliminate these factors.

Faulty habits and patterns developed through our formative years

A major factor in our gradual physical development during the formative years from birth to physical maturity is the period from crawling to erect posture, when we learn new skills, including balance and walking, the activation of neural pathways for posture, and a variety of innumerable new movement sequence patterns.

Many influences can result in faulty habits with posture, balance, coordination, shallow breathing, muscle tension, negative attitudes, thoughts, and feelings. When a neural pathway is activated, there is a tendency to utilise this same pathway; this could appear to be the beginning of forming faulty habits with the development of muscular and structural imbalances as well as uncoordinated movement sequences. When muscle testing, it is common to find that a child's self-image has been negatively affected during these early formative years.

All people develop muscular imbalances from childhood and throughout their lives. The imbalanced muscular movement creates strengths and weaknesses. For example, the body's natural response—to settle in a comfortable position—creates an imbalance elsewhere.

Similarly, a sprained right ankle in childhood has the potential to cause overall muscular imbalances when the body naturally and subconsciously switches weight, balance, and reliance to the left ankle. Even after the injury has repaired, the body will favour the left ankle as habit—and a negative new muscle memory is formed.

There are situations that can cause muscular imbalances. Therefore, when assessing someone for the first time, it is expected that most of the following common and detrimental factors that adversely affect the body will be present:

- Impairment of the sacral and coccygeal nerves
- Misalignments of the spinal column and overall skeletal structure
- Muscular imbalances
- Uncoordinated movement sequence patterns
- Stress and stress patterns
- Breathing that is not in synchronisation with overall body function
- Extreme changes in weather temperatures that adversely affect the body
- Various airborne pollutants carried by winds around the world
- Negative attitudes, thoughts, feelings, and emotions
- Prostheses and scar tissue that can cause blockages in energy flow
- Self-image and its self-limiting parameters
- Eye movements that cause muscular weakness

The truly outstanding feature of this program is that in one session of approximately an hour, the VET self-help breathing techniques can be demonstrated to correct and eliminate these common detrimental factors. These VET techniques also correct neurological dysfunctions and overall muscular or skeletal imbalances in the body. The marked improvement immediately becomes evident after the use of each technique. In fact, each of these corrections can be made in just a few minutes; the purpose of the initial demonstration is to explain and to commence teaching the VET techniques.

Testing and assessment

Within a few minutes, the overall condition of the body can be tested and assessed for any common detrimental factors and muscular and skeletal imbalances. These factors adversely affect performance and predispose the body to illnesses and injuries. Corrections are made on the treatment table as well as in the sitting and standing positions. The overall condition is also assessed and corrected after walking or running and a variety of other movement sequences. After using these techniques to remove these common detrimental factors and thereby relieve overall muscular imbalances, the body immediately functions at a much higher level of efficiency.

The mind-brain-body is multidimensional, functioning at many different levels or frequencies beyond the physical level. The body's life force energy circuitry is electromagnetic in nature.

Testing is carried out with the person on the treatment table in the supine (face up) position. The purpose of this testing is twofold: to quickly assess a person's condition and then to demonstrate the immediate and overall beneficial improvement that occurs with VET techniques.

Muscle testing as an aid to diagnosis

With every patient tested through my years in clinical practice, I would explain how this muscle testing procedure functioned. This has been appreciated by everyone and has given people confidence and a greater understanding of what is happening overall in the body.

The next test is with the person in the face down, or prone, position. Testing in this position includes applying traction to both legs to check the difference, if any, in leg lengths, misalignment of the spine and pelvis and the occipital condyles of the skull. There will be misalignment of the whole spine and pelvis with this testing. With equal traction applied to both legs, it appears as if there is a difference in leg lengths, and this is usually caused by the overall imbalance of the musculature of the body. Only rarely is there an actual anatomical difference in the length of both legs. Such anatomical differences could perhaps be caused by bone fractures or with hip replacement, when the surgeon has decided it is beneficial to have a slight difference in length because of the overall adaptation of the body.

Self-help techniques

- Breathing techniques (see chapters 2 and 5).
- Arm-swinging exercises to develop overall coordination with movement to ensure that

the corresponding joints in the arms and legs are coordinated and move in synchronization. For example, if the body is viewed from a different perspective with a person being on all fours and functioning as a quadruped, then feet correspond with hands, ankles with wrists, calves with forearms, knees with elbows, and hips with shoulders. These simple arm-swinging exercises make overall corrections in the body. In chapter 7, an analogy of coiled springs at each joint is presented. The body would be thrown out of balance if one spring is strong and its corresponding spring is weak at the same joint.

- The art of relaxation, revitalization, and goal-setting visualization.
- Facilitating the learning and development of new skills.
- Coordinating and synchronizing overall muscle function with walking and a wide variety of movement sequences.
- Removing the self-limiting parameters of a negative self-image and developing a positive new self-image.
- Techniques to activate new neural pathways to make specific corrections.

Our innate feelings—an integral part of healthy mind-brain-body function Comfort and security, enjoyment and pleasure, control, love and gratitude, expression

With our Vortex Energy Therapy program, the effects of our innate feelings on body function can be demonstrated. Furthermore, it can explain how these feelings are produced and how the functioning of each feeling requires a specific frequency of electromagnetic life force energy.

Specific feelings are an integral part of the mind-brain-body function. The innate feelings that play an important role to ensure a healthy and balanced mind, brain, and body are feeling comfortable and secure; enjoying pleasurable sensual feelings, with touch, taste, hearing, sight, and smell; being in control of one's self; and feeling loved and grateful in reciprocating that love towards others. Enjoying, experiencing, and expressing these feelings plays an important role in mind-brain-body function and serves as a survival mechanism in the body.

Affirmations that include the body's innate feelings are powerful and produce immediate and overall beneficial effects in the body. Daily affirmations guide us in achieving our goals, keep us focused, and change our attitudes. Perhaps you already have you own favourite affirmations that you enjoy. If so, that's great. If not, here is a suggested affirmation verse that includes the innate feelings that are important for mind-brain-body function. It is my first attempt at composing a little verse. I hope it sounds right for you.

With feelings of love, kindness, caring, and gratitude,
I am enriching my life by improving my attitude.
I am breathing in the energy to ensure
I feel calm, comfortable, confident, secure,
In control at all times, in every situation,
Revitalizing with breathing and relaxation.

Enthusiastic, energetic, enjoying life, having fun,
With dear friends I care for, each and every one.
I am enriching my life by improving my attitude,
With feelings of love, kindness, caring, and gratitude.
—Allan

There may be one or two lines that appeal to you more than the others do. If so, then use those thoughts and feelings as your affirmations more often. But of course, the entire affirmation verse is well worthwhile, producing beneficial effects.

Chapter 2

Visualizing How the Techniques Are So Effective

As well as enjoying good health and well-being and becoming capable of performing at your potential, the purpose of the program is to assist with self-development in achieving your objectives by using self-help techniques, breathing, movement, relaxation, revitalization, and goal-setting visualization.

The main aim of this program is to balance posture and to coordinate and synchronize the overall musculature of the body with movement. How pleasing it is to be able to test and confirm with muscle testing the immediate beneficial changes that have occurred after the use of VET techniques. In balancing the posture, the aim is to ensure that the body's centre of gravity line runs through the body's weight-bearing joints of the spine and is also parallel with the femur and tibia bones. It is the overall balancing of the musculature of the body that aligns the whole structure. The balanced muscular tilt of the pelvis and also the skull determines the desirable relaxed, balanced, and erect posture. This is also explained briefly in chapter 6.

The main principle of Vortex Energy Therapy to be remembered is that the mind-brain-body is comprised of a series of systems designed to function in harmony and synchronization as integral parts of a whole unit. Explaining how the Vortex Energy Therapy self-help breathing techniques function is an excellent example of this principle. It explains how the respiratory system functions in combination and synchronization with all other bodily systems as integral parts of the whole mind-brain-body. This explanation continues in chapter 5.

A picture is worth a thousand words.

Similarly, with presentations and demonstrations of our Vortex Energy Therapy (VET) program, everyone can see the immediate beneficial improvements in the body, the correction and elimination of overall misalignments, the balancing and coordination of the muscles with posture and movements, all happening with just a simple breathing or other Vortex Energy Therapy self-help technique. It's exciting to see the immediate results.

With explanations and testing the results, seeing the effectiveness from the use of self-help techniques each time, it certainly gives confidence and encouragement to know that it is well worthwhile to use and experience these techniques. More importantly, if you picture in your imagination and visualize what happens every time with each technique, you will have a much broader understanding of mind-brain-body function and understand the reason that the techniques produce such beneficial results.

This is what I would like to share with you on this exciting journey. This chapter gives a summary of the self-help techniques. Any repetition will serve as a worthwhile purpose of being reminded and assist with imprinting the techniques in your mind.

Summary of self-help techniques

This section presents an overview of the self-help techniques in the whole program.

Introducing the Vortex Energy Therapy breathing techniques

Why is it that VET breathing techniques are so effective in producing immediate and overall beneficial results? The lungs function as a part of the respiratory system in combination and synchronization with all other bodily systems, all functioning in response to the demands or bodily requirements placed on the respiratory system, particularly from muscular exertion. The reason that the breathing techniques are so effective with overall corrections in the body is because of the movement along the spine, which involves the respiratory, neurological, and musculoskeletal systems in addition to all other bodily systems functioning together in combination. The movement along the spine can be quite subtle yet produce immediate overall beneficial results and corrections.

When breathing in, it is the arching of the lower back that causes movement along the spine. The lifting and then rolling back of the shoulders opens and expands the upper regions of the lungs and activates the intercostal muscles and all the muscles of inspiration and expiration. Breathing is effortless. It is the movement that causes expansion of the lungs.

With the VET breathing techniques, breathing is always in and out through the nostrils with the mouth closed. It is this overall involvement of all bodily systems functioning in combination and synchronization as an integrated whole unit that makes the needed corrections throughout the body.

Posture balancing

When testing anyone for the first time, it is most common to find that there is an overall imbalance of the whole musculature of the body, especially with the anterior and posterior muscles in the sitting and standing positions. As mentioned previously, this has most likely been the situation since early childhood in the formative years, from crawling to the upright posture and walking. It is a most difficult situation for anyone to be able to achieve a balanced, relaxed, and erect posture because the neural pathways for good posture have most likely not been activated in the early formative years.

Over a period of time, people adapt to the postures that are comfortable for them. They also adapt to different postures because of the effects of different traumas that have occurred to them during the years. It would be difficult for most people to change from such states because of the overall muscular imbalances that have occurred through the years with adaptation.

The VET techniques facilitate the restoration of good posture by activating the neural pathways for a balanced and relaxed posture. In one session, the immediate beneficial effects can be experienced, observed, explained, and demonstrated with each technique.

States of mind—developing awareness

This section, a most important part of the Vortex Energy Therapy program, develops awareness of different states of mind that have been classified into four categories:

- A mind occupied with common negative thoughts, attitudes, feelings and emotions.
- A mind with restricting attitudes and obstacles to learning, communicating, and development.
- A mind without negative or restrictive attitudes but constantly thinking, reasoning, and asking questions, not pausing to listen and be open-minded and receptive to one's thoughts, when often ideas come from the subconscious mind or higher levels of consciousness, to solve or to create.
- Calmness of mind and being open-minded, unbiased or unprejudiced, increasing awareness and understanding, developing positive thoughts, attitudes, and feelings, such as love, gratitude, friendship, caring, and enthusiasm. Feeling comfortable, confident, and secure, in control at all times and enjoying life. Clearing the mind of conscious thinking and then listening to hear and to heed thoughts, ideas, and solutions that come when the mind is open. What is it we want

to know? We need to ask the questions and then listen to the thoughts that come in reply. This is the level of creativity and innovation.

If we want to change, we need to become aware of our thoughts, feelings, attitudes, habits, and emotions. We could begin by asking, "What is my attitude? Is it negative or positive?" Chapter 10 presents these states of mind and include depicting diagrams.

Egotism, meaning to be excessively conceited or absorbed in oneself, is a major factor hindering healing, health, well-being, and clarity of thought.

A guided relaxation, revitalization, and goal-setting visualization session

We will be discussing how to instantly relax, communicate with your body, breathe energy into your body, and learn the locations of the main sets of vortexes and the colours, musical notes, and feelings associated with each vortex. In this beautiful calm state, visualize yourself as you would like to be and see yourself achieving the goals that you have set.

And of course, it should be added that this relaxation session is intended to revitalize and reenergize your whole body. The art of instant relaxation is to just close your eyes and to perceive and feel your breath as it comes through your nostrils. You just let the breath come into your body automatically. Put yourself on autopilot and keep perceiving your breath as you inhale and exhale, as well as the rise and fall of your chest as you let it sink into a deeper state of relaxation with each exhalation. This relaxation session is explained in more detail in chapter 8.

The memories of stressful situations may have been forgotten, but the adverse effects of such stress become evident with overall muscular imbalances, weaknesses, structural misalignments, and neurological dysfunctions, with muscles not functioning in coordination. The body reveals a most common overall phenomenon that I have termed a "stress pattern." This is described in chapter 9. There are many aspects about stress in other chapters to develop awareness of stress and ensure that the body remains stress-free. How the Vortex Energy Therapy techniques correct and eliminate stress can be demonstrated.

The body in motion

With walking, running, playing sports, and other activities, the VET techniques facilitate the development of a relaxed, rhythmical ease of movement as well as overall balance in the body. This approach ensures the overall balance, coordination, and synchronization of muscle and joint function in the arms and legs. It could be said that this is perfection with movement.

To have a better understanding, the body is viewed from the perspective of being on all fours, hands and feet. Chapter 7 explains the method to achieve this high level of efficiency and performance. When initially testing anyone, it has been found that apart from the muscle function, the movements at the joints are not propelling the body with similar force. An analogy to describe this would be to imagine a strong coiled spring at one knee joint and a weak coiled spring at the other. It then becomes obvious how this difference would cause overall imbalance in the body. The VET techniques correct all these imbalances in one session. The arm-swinging exercises with paper drumsticks ensure that the body's overall balance, coordination, and the synchronicity of movement with the corresponding joints is maintained.

Self-image

Self-image is the perception one has of one's abilities, appearance, and personality. With an initial testing, it can be demonstrated that a negative self-image is similar to a stress pattern in that it is submerged in the mind at a subconscious level. It will retard or hinder an individual from performing or achieving beyond the restricting limitations of this self-image, even though consciously there is a strong desire to achieve some particular goals.

It can be demonstrated how self-help breathing techniques will immediately correct and remove these restricting parameters. Setting a vibrant, wholesome new image of yourself can be a part of your relaxation and visualization sessions. It is only natural to sometimes have doubts, frustration, fears, irritations, anxiety, and so forth, but when you become aware of what is happening, just think and feel love and gratitude. These powerful feelings will immediately remove any adverse effects and radiate out from your body.

Facilitating the learning and development of new skills with VET techniques

Remember that the VET techniques balance and coordinate the whole body to function at its highest level of efficiency. Then the techniques activate neural pathways that are specific for the movements of the new skills. The objective with the learning and development of new skills is to reach the stage of performing the skills automatically, without consciously thinking about the movement.

For example, with touch typing, you are focusing on the words to express yourself and what you want to write, without thinking about which fingers to use with each key. Playing the piano is another similar example, with the fingers moving over the keyboard to play the correct notes without consciously thinking about your fingers. Remember the old adage that practice makes perfect? But beware of practising mistakes and faulty habits.

Competent coaching is certainly important and worthwhile. Of course some coaches have their limitations. Observing the skills being performed to imprint the movements in one's mind and then using the VET techniques to activate the neural pathways for these movements will facilitate the learning process when combined with practice.

Dancing

Is there any other pastime more enjoyable and exhilarating than dancing? There is such a diverse variety of movement sequence patterns, especially with ballroom dancing. In learning, there are so many aspects to be considered, with new routines, steps, skills, posture, balance, coordination, and feelings while being in harmony with your partner, and most importantly, dancing in time with the music.

The VET techniques correct all of these aspects after first using techniques to bring mind-brain-body function to its potential. Techniques also facilitate the learning by activating the neural pathways for all new movement sequence patterns. By observing with guided commentary the actual performances that you would like to emulate, you become aware of what is not known about the new skills. This could be through watching videos, DVDs, and so forth, to mentally imprint a variety of movement sequence patterns.

Then you practise, practise, practise each movement with guidance from a competent coach or teacher. Your approach will be greatly enhanced and facilitated by using these techniques before you commence learning these new skills.

Adapting to a change of pace or tempo to overcome any weakening effects

How enjoyable it was to be at the 1956 Melbourne Olympics and to see Volodymyr Kuts win the 10,000 metres using tactics that became known as "surging," which is varying the pace with sudden, extreme changes of pace. Having broken the world record in Moscow two months earlier, he was considered to be favourite for this event. Gordon Pirie was also considered to have a possibility of winning the gold medal because he had previously beaten Vladimir Kuts in the 5000 metre event in England two months earlier.

It was an amazing race! Kuts raced the first lap in only 61.2 seconds and ran so quickly in the first half of the race that he almost passed Emil Zatopek's Olympic record for 5000 metres and he still had another 5000 metres to run. Throughout the race, he would sprint and then slow down, moving to the outside and waving to Pirie to pass him, but Pirie preferred to remain at his shoulder. Eventually, Pirie was forced to take the lead because Kuts stopped so suddenly. Kuts then relaxed his pace for the next half a lap, and then, with a sudden burst of speed, he again took the lead to go on to win the gold medal.

The reason for relating this story about Volodymyr Kuts and his surging change of pace is to say how tiring and demanding these changes are, which would have a weakening effect on most runners or any sports people. But it is important to mention that with our VET program, there is a technique to correct and eliminate these adverse effects so that a change of pace does not cause any weakening. Perhaps these techniques would also prove to be most beneficial with many sports and activities such as soccer, hockey, football, ballroom dancing, and so on, where there is a sudden change of pace or tempo. It would certainly be a worthwhile project to test this change of pace aspect.

From resting in bed or on the couch to sitting and standing

I have found that when testing a person who moves from reclining on the bed or couch to sitting on the side to then standing, there is weakening of an indicator testing muscle. It seems apparent that there is a need to activate the neural pathways for these movements. This situation immediately changes when the person performs a simple VET breathing technique and the person tests strong.

This discovery is of paramount importance particularly with elderly people, who find difficulty when adapting to the erect posture after sitting. This technique is explained in chapter 6, "Posture Balancing and Coordinated Movement," and also in chapter 7, "The Body in Motion."

Chapter 3

The Structure of Vortex Energy Therapy

Vortex Energy Therapy is a correlation and a merging of the ancient knowledge of the East—from China, India, Japan, and Thailand—with the neurological, musculoskeletal, anatomical aspects of Western science. Although this ancient Eastern knowledge has led to many exciting ground breaking discoveries with improving mind-brain-body function, the Vortex Energy Therapy self-help techniques, with breathing, movement, and so forth, are unique and completely different from any of these ancient practices.

The structure or basis on which VET has been developed is a combination and correlation of the following:

- The meridian system, or theory of the channels, which is the basis or circuitry of Traditional Chinese Medicine and utilized in the practice of acupuncture (China)
- The chakras, nadi, subtle bodies, the basis of the ancient practice of yoga (India)
- The neurological, musculoskeletal, and anatomical structure of the body

Testing the knowledge of the above-mentioned practices, in combination and in parallel, reaffirms and authenticates the chakras and meridians as being an integral part of mind-brain-body function.

This knowledge has been integrated, correlated, and used in a completely different approach in combination with the neurological and musculoskeletal aspects of mind-brain-body function, forming the multidimensional structure of the Vortex Energy Therapy system and program.

In chapter 5, "Balance and Revitalize Your Body," there is no longer any mention of the chakras, energy channels, or the meridian system. At this stage with breathing techniques, the focus is on the neurological and musculoskeletal aspects of the body, the spine, the nervous system, the spinal cord, the nerve plexuses, the endocrine system, the respiratory system, the muscular system, the genitourinary system, and all other bodily systems functioning in synchronization as integral parts of a whole unit, the mind-brain-body.

The significance of the chakras (vortexes) with mind-brain-body function

Although I had practised yoga with two excellent teachers whose emphasis was on the breathing and exercise aspects, there was little awareness, if any, on my part, about the chakras being such an integral part of mind-brain-body function. For without the chakras there would not be any mind-brain-body function.

Discovering the significance of the chakras or vortexes was a major breakthrough with testing. Providence then seemed to lead me on an exciting journey. My first thoughts were to focus on learning as much as possible about the chakras. My first step was to test and correlate the chakras or vortexes with the nervous system. Which segments of the spine and the nervous system corresponded with each of the seven main chakras? It soon became evident that each chakra corresponded with each of the nerve plexuses as well as the endocrine system. It became such a fascinating study, with information gleaned from many sources, especially with testing, to discover and locate vortexes around, above, and below the body.

What do we understand about the chakras?

In the practice of yoga, a chakra is described as a spinning vortex of energy. The word *chakra* comes from the Sanskrit word for "wheel" or "disk." Vortex, as you may know, is an English word meaning "a whirling mass, especially a whirlpool or a whirlwind." Have you watched, studied, and wondered about the vortex as you emptied the water from your washbasin, sink, or bath? Does this vortex of water whirl around clockwise or anticlockwise as it empties from the outlet pipe? Energy is developed within the water in this way.

Within our systems, the vortexes (or vortices) have been utilized in a different and unique way from the chakras in the practice of yoga, hence our name Vortex Energy Therapy, to avoid confusion with any other system, practice, or modality. As well as that, the diagrams and charts of our VET system illustrate and utilize in practice many sets of vortexes and overlapping sets functioning at different levels or frequencies.

It is not necessary to learn in detail about the meridian system and the vortexes.

The main requirement of the VET program is to learn, understand, and use the self-help techniques. With simple self-help breathing, movement, relaxation, goal setting, and visualization techniques, everyone can enjoy better health and well-being, become balanced, and be capable of performing at one's potential without studying in detail about the meridian system and the vortexes.

Initially it was intended to explain briefly about the entire functioning of the meridian system, with diagrams showing the course of the meridians. Rather than do this, with the possibility of causing confusion, it is better that the focus is relevant to and confined to the objectives of our program.

For anyone who is interested, it is worthwhile to explain how the two systems correlate. The knowledge of the vortexes will come easily because it is all incorporated into the program. My good friends Margaret and Michael Cavanagh provided the analogy that you do not have to be a mechanic to drive a car, but it is certainly worthwhile to have some knowledge of the car to ensure that the engine is fine-tuned and running smoothly.

From testing through the years, here is my perception of the meridian system, which has, as already stated, been correlated and used in combination in a different manner with the vortexes (the chakras in the practice of yoga) and tested in parallel with the neurological and musculoskeletal aspects of the body. Instead of speaking of the flow of the chi energy through the channels and balancing this chi life force energy, as is the practice in Traditional Chinese Medicine, this circuitry, with the VET program, is viewed as being an electromagnetic circuitry and multidimensional in that it functions at many different levels or frequencies beyond the physical level of the body.

The meridians are the main trunks and course lengthwise through the body. The collaterals are the interconnecting branches between one channel and another. The whole channel system is classified into two groups: the regular channels, known as the "'Twelve Channels". The extra channels, known as the "'Eight Extra Channels'

The Twelve Channels

The Twelve Channels, or meridians, in their course of circulation, connect superficially with the upper and lower extremities, head and trunk and internally with the viscera and are named after the organ with which each meridian connects, except for the triple heater meridian, which functions as a thermostat to assist the body in adapting to changes in the weather temperature. The meridians also connect the upper, middle, and lower portions of the body.

In the hands, information can be accessed from points on each of the fingers regarding their corresponding meridians: lung, large intestine, heart, small intestine, pericardium, and triple heater. There are yin and yang meridians that finish and commence near the tips of the fingers. There are also pulse points located on each wrist, through which information can be accessed about each meridian and the condition of the body.

In the feet, information can be accessed from each of the toes regarding the other meridians: stomach, spleen, urinary bladder, kidney, gall bladder, and liver meridians. In accessing information from the fingers and toes, it also immediately provides much information about the overall condition of the body.

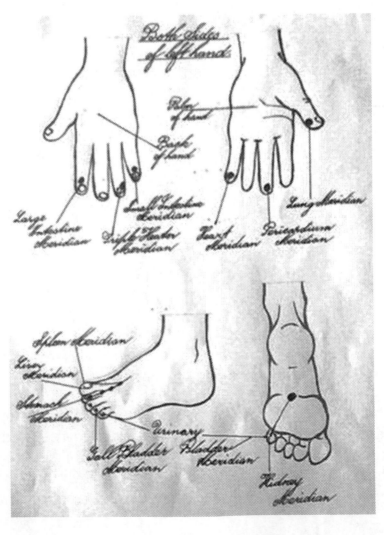

For example, using the VET program when initially testing anyone, the heart meridian point at the tip of the little finger will cause an indicator testing muscle to weaken in revealing a common phenomenon that I have termed a stress pattern, as further described in chapter 9. This immediately provides information about the overall structural misalignments, muscular imbalances, and weaknesses in the body. Similarly with the triple heater meridian, the point at the outer edge of the nail of the ring finger provides information about the overall imbalances and adverse effects in the body, caused by extreme changes in weather temperature.

Information can be quickly assessed about many common detrimental factors predisposing the body to injuries and illnesses, also serving as a hindrance to performing at one's potential. For example, with athletes, footballers, or anyone involved in sports, information can be quickly determined about anyone who is predisposed to injuries. The whole program is about so much more than simply discovering deficiencies with energy flow in each of the meridians. The VET techniques correct and eliminate all these adverse factors in bringing the mind-brain-body to function with maximal efficiency, enabling anyone to become capable of performing at his or her potential.

The Eight Extra Channels

In the front of the body, there is the Ren channel or Front Midline channel. At the back of the body there is the Du channel or Back Midline channel. There are points or miniature vortexes, along both of these channels or meridians. The other extra channels or meridians do not have points of their own but share points with the other meridians. They include vital channel, belt channel, regulating channel of yin, regulating channel of yang, motility channel of yin, and motility channel of yang.

The vortexes function in combination with the meridian system. Spaced along each meridian are a series of points which are stimulated in the practice of acupuncture, shiatsu etc. These points are in fact miniature vortexes.

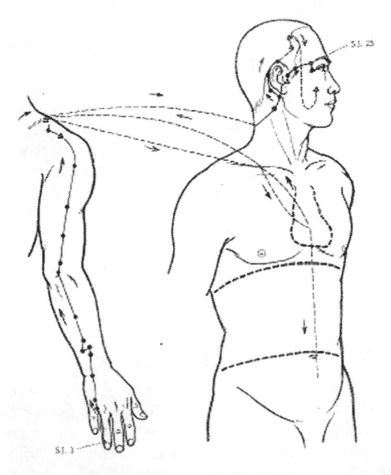

Fig. 17. The Sanjiao Channel of Hand-Shaoyang

The triple heater or triple warmer meridian.

Triple Heater	
Upper Warmer	Head, heart, and lungs
Middle Warmer	Digestive system
Lower Warmer	Kidneys, lower intestines and reproductive system

The triple heater acts as the body's thermostat. When the energy in the upper warmer becomes overheated affecting the head, heart, and lungs, the triple heater circulates heat down through the middle to the lower warmer, where the hot energy is cooled and then recirculated back to the head, heart, and lungs to help in cooling these organs. The hot energy also prevents the lower energies from becoming too cold.

It can be demonstrated that sudden extreme changes in the weather temperature cause overall imbalances and dysfunctions that can be corrected with VET techniques. When making corrections, the Chong Mai channel, or vital channel meridian, which plays an important role with the external environment and circulation, is also checked and corrected.

Externally the body can be detrimentally affected by such factors as extreme changes in weather temperature, winds carrying airborne pollutants, fire, and other phenomena of nature. Diseases caused by these phenomena of nature are known as exogenous diseases.

Internally the body can be adversely affected by emotional stress factors such as anger, anxiety, sadness, grief, fear, and so on. Ailments caused by these factors are known as endogenous factors.

My perception of mind-brain-body function— culminating from over thirty-seven years of research

With testing through the years and being fortunate to be able to study many systems and modalities from around the world, with information coming from numerous sources, here briefly is my perception of mind-brain-body function.

The mind-brain-body consists of a vast network of life force energy circuits, electromagnetic in nature and multidimensional, in that this circuitry functions at many different levels or frequencies beyond the physical level. This electromagnetic life force energy comes into the body from the earth and the universe through a series of vortexes that function as vital energy centres and step-down transformers to transform this electromagnetic energy to levels or frequencies suitable for mind-brain-body function.

Discovering the many levels of Vortex Energy Therapy

With this whole research program, discovering the many levels of our Vortex Energy Therapy system has been an exciting journey for me. The different levels include an emotional level, mental level, hormonal level, causal level, left brain, right brain, male and female circuitries, and many more that can be tapped into. But the most exciting and ground-breaking discovery is the mind-brain-body level, which is the body's control centre, functioning as a marvellous biological computer. At this level, information can be obtained about the overall condition of the body, including new information about the vertebral column, the spinal cord and nervous system, and the sacral and coccygeal nerves. These are outstanding discoveries because it is only at this level that this information is evident.

The energy fields surrounding the body

Surrounding the physical body is a large energy field referred to in Eastern texts as the soul body. Then beyond this energy field, there is an all-embracing energy field referred to in Eastern texts as the spiritual body. With testing through the years, these large energy fields are checked, assessed, and used in making any necessary corrections, confirming their authenticity. Within these large energy fields are vortexes that transform the life force energy to levels suitable for mind-body function. With testing, we are able to access these large energy fields to assess any adverse effects that are happening at the physical level. Correction can be made at these higher levels with these connections to the physical level.

The corresponding locations of the vortexes on the body

First Vortex	Hands, feet, and coccygeal region
Second Vortex	Wrists, ankles, and pubic region
Third Vortex	Diaphragm, forearms, and calves
Fourth Vortex	Mid chest, elbows, and knees
Fifth Vortex	Throat, shoulders, hips, and pelvis

It is worthwhile to become aware of these locations, because in chapter 7, "The Body in Motion," the body is viewed from a different perspective, as being on all fours, hands and feet. It then becomes more obvious how to balance the body with movement by synchronizing the vortexes.

The chart presented below was developed by Allan Warrener as a result of his research with the Vortex Energy Therapy program.

Locations of the Vortexes

VORTEX	V First Set Location	VL Second Set Location	VA Third Set Location	VO Fourth Set (overlapping) Location	VS Fifth Set (overlapping) Location All-embracing Energy Field	Colour	Feelings	Musical Note
First	Coccygeal region	Feet	Hands	Feet and ankles	Approximately two feet below feet	Red	Comfort Security	C
Second	Pubic region Ovaries Testes	Ankles	Wrists	Knees to ankles	Above knees, (i.e., external to body)	Orange	Pleasure Enjoyment	D
Third	Diaphragm	Calves	Forearms	Knees to thigh	Above diaphragm(i.e., external to body)	Yellow	Control	E
Fourth	Mid Sternum	Knees	Elbows	Pelvic girdle	Approximately six inches above head	Green	Love Kindness Friendship	F
Fifth	Throat	Pelvis	Shoulders	Whole abdominal region to neck	Approximately two feet above head	Blue	Expression Fulfilment	G
Sixth	Forehead	Forehead	Forehead	Forehead	Approximately four feet above head	Indigo	Intuition	A
Seventh	Crown	Crown	Crown	Crown	Approximately six feet above head	Violet	Spiritual	B

Remember, these vortexes act as step-down transformers to transform the life force and electromagnetic energy to levels suitable for mind-brain-body function. Balancing the corresponding vortexes balances and coordinates the whole body with movement, as explained in chapter 7, "The Body in Motion.

Note: There is an overlapping set on the body and another set in the large overall embracing energy field surrounding the body. The vortexes spin or whirl clockwise and anticlockwise alternatively as each one next to the other is located in the body. The spinning is opposite in male and female. The directions of spinning with each of the corresponding male and female vortexes are opposite, clockwise, and anticlockwise, as listed below.

Locations of the vortexes and the direction of spiralling.	Female	Male
First – Coccygeal region, base of the spine	Clockwise	Anticlockwise
Second – Pubic region, (ovaries, testes)	Anticlockwise	Clockwise
Third – Diaphragm	Clockwise	Anticlockwise
Fourth – Mid chest	Anticlockwise	Clockwise
Fifth – Throat	Clockwise	Anticlockwise
Sixth – Forehead	Anticlockwise	Clockwise
Seventh – Crown of head	Clockwise	Anticlockwise

Chapter 4

The Mind-Brain-Body Biological Computer

As you are probably aware, the brain communicates with the whole body through the nervous system, both at a conscious and subconscious level. The autonomic nervous system is that part of the nervous system not consciously directed, which regulates and controls all bodily functions, such as circulation, digestion, and so on. The central nervous system functions at a conscious level and includes parts of the brain concerned with consciousness and mental activities, the spinal cord, sensory and motor nerve fibres, which control the skeletal muscles.

As the nervous system is an extension of the brain and communicates with every part of the body, let us call the nervous system by another name, the brain's communicating circuitry. If we are touched on any part of the body, immediately we are able to recognize where we are being touched and the type of touch. We can then appreciate that the mind, brain, and body are intimately connected.

These facts are only presented here as a reminder of how the mind is connected with the body through the nervous system, both at a subconscious level and conscious level, and to remind ourselves of the influence of thoughts and feelings on bodily functions. With the learning of new skills, the movement commences with thoughts and visualization of the movements to be performed. With much practice and repetition as these skills are learnt, the neural pathways for these movements can be activated, so eventually a stage can be reached where the new skills are performed automatically, without much conscious thought. Learning new skills can certainly take a lengthy period of time. It is also a period when many faulty habits from early childhood can develop from the early formative years.

The Vortex Energy Therapy (VET) techniques activate the neural pathways to facilitate the learning of new movement sequence patterns with the learning of new skills. The techniques also correct the faulty habits from the early formative years as well as many other common detrimental factors. For example, if you would like to learn to dance the tango, you could watch dancers whom you would like to emulate, performing it to imprint the movements in your mind. Then using the VET techniques, the neural pathways for these movement sequence patterns can be activated to facilitate learning any new steps.

The overall functioning of the mind, brain, and body can be envisaged as a biological computer, presenting us with a multidimensional life force energy circuitry, electromagnetic in nature, functioning at many levels or different frequencies—a vast, precisely structured circuitry with seemingly unlimited possibilities of new discoveries for anyone involved in different areas of research.

The information and development of the whole Vortex Energy Therapy structured circuitry and program eventuated as a result of searching for the causes of various ailments and injuries to help patients.

Although it is exciting to relate these discoveries, it is important for us not to lose sight of our objectives and to focus on our VET self-help techniques with breathing, movement, relaxation, revitalization, and goal-setting visualization.

Different forms of muscle testing are presented briefly only for the information of anyone who is interested. It is not a requirement of our Vortex Energy Therapy program to understand how to muscle test.

How can information about the overall condition of the body be assessed?

Touch computer screen

The whole body's surface can be visualized as a touch computer screen, with many points overall through which we are able to access information and assess bodily functions. This is done by the practitioner touching these points located on the body's surface with one hand or finger, while at the same time testing a muscle, chosen as being suitable to use as an indicator testing muscle with the other hand. In making contact with both hands, the practitioner forms an arc or complete circuit. For example, if the patient's right arm has been chosen as an indicator testing muscle then the practitioner uses his or her left hand to apply resistance and test strength while at the same time touching a specific body point. If the indicator testing muscle weakens, it indicates that there is a break in the body's electromagnetic life force energy within this particular circuit. The numerous body points each provide information about the body's condition.

With the diagram in chapter 3, "The Structure of Vortex Energy Therapy," you will notice that the twelve meridians course to the fingers and toes. Although there are many points on the body through which information can be accessed, the fingers and toes can quickly provide information of any blockages in any of the meridians. For example, when testing anyone for the first time, there will be a stress pattern, and it can be confidently predicted that there are overall structural misalignments and muscular imbalances, with the muscles not functioning in coordination and synchronization with movement. As well as this, there are detrimental effects with functional physiology. These adverse effects can be predicted because of stress and stress patterns. The stress pattern phenomenon is explained in chapter 9, "Stress and Stress Patterns."

Dr George Goodheart, a chiropractor who developed the therapeutic system known as Applied Kinesiology discovered that it was possible to access information about the body with muscle testing. He used this approach in combination with other neurological and orthopaedic tests as an aid to diagnosis. Health practitioners around the world have been using this form of muscle testing for many years, also as an aid to diagnosis. Body points vary with different therapeutic systems in accessing information about the various aspects of the body's condition. Many colleagues I know have studied more than one therapeutic system or modality, such as Applied Kinesiology, Total Body Modification, Neural Organizational Techniques, and so forth. Although the information sought with each of these systems is different and the body points may differ, the principle with muscle testing to access information in this way should be the same approach.

With the VET program, although innumerable points can be accessed at multidimensional levels, the program has been simplified, which has resulted in an overall assessment being made through a smaller number of points. Using the VET approach, accessing information and making corrections is not a time-consuming procedure.

Touching the different points on the body combined with muscle testing enables us to communicate with this marvellous mind-brain-body biological computer. It enables us to locate any dysfunctional breaks in the body's electromagnetic life force energy circuitry. It is telling your body that these are the dysfunctional points where you would like to restore life force energy flow. It seems that any dysfunctional circuitry registers within the brain as a result of this touching. It then happens that the VET breathing techniques or other VET techniques make the overall corrections in the body because the respiratory system is functioning in synchronization with all other bodily systems as an integrated whole unit.

Hocus-pocus, mumbo jumbo, or gobbledegook?

The art of muscle testing as an aid to diagnosis, used in combination with neurological and orthopaedic tests—how to use this form of muscle testing

This form of muscle testing as an aid to diagnosis is explained for the benefit of practitioners and therapists who may not be aware of it but are familiar with the neurological and orthopaedic form of muscle testing. For some, it could seem like a lot of hocus-pocus, mumbo-jumbo, or gobbledegook, so any scepticism is quite understandable. The art of this form of muscle testing is part of our Vortex Energy Therapy program for any practitioners who are interested. With knowledge of the various body points, much information can be accurately accessed and assessed within a few minutes.

For example, by just touching one body point, overall information about the whole body is immediately known. Through my years in clinical practice, most patients appreciated having it explained to them and had a good understanding of the whole procedure. Often I would ask a patient, "What's the problem?" The reply would often be, "You tell me." So it was reassuring to be able to use muscle testing to accurately provide so much information to the person about the overall condition of the body, much more than he or she imagined.

Muscle testing as an aid to diagnosis

So let us explain this art of muscle testing as an aid to diagnosis. This has been my approach through the years when testing a patient's overall condition. Assuming that we are using the muscles of the patient's right arm as a group of indicator testing muscles in order to access and assess information. The patient on the couch or being tested on the treatment table, in the supine position (face up), holds his or her right arm rigidly locked at an angle of about thirty degrees laterally to the body. I would usually explain it to everyone this way: "Imagine you are standing and holding a bucket of water with your arm straight, approximately thirty degrees away from your body, and hold your arm in that position without trying to lift your arm to raise the bucket of water. With my left hand I would then apply resistant pressure against the arm just above the wrist. The patient does not attempt to move his or her arm against this resistance but just holds the arm firmly in place against resistance.

If there is a break in the life force energy electromagnetic circuitry caused by the practitioner touching a particular point on the body with his or her other hand, then the indicator muscles will weaken.

In using both hands with testing, the practitioner forms an arc, or a complete circuit. This is how information can be accessed from the body. The practitioner does not attempt to overpower the person being tested but simply applies a strong resistance, which is held briefly, for about one second. For example, the practitioner says "hold" and then both the practitioner and patient relax their arms after a brief one-second resistance. The practitioner relaxes his or her arm first.

Testing to obtain information is only explained for the benefit of anyone who has not been made aware of this method to access information in combination with other neurological and orthopaedic tests. It is truly an art that requires teaching and guidance.

Neurological and orthopaedic muscle testing

How does muscle testing as an aid to diagnosis differ from neurological and orthopaedic muscle testing as used when conducting medical testing procedures? With neurological and orthopaedic muscle testing, assuming that a particular muscle—for example, the deltoid—is being tested, then the focus with testing would be with this muscle in isolation. In this case the examiner's resistance would be against the elbow in order to only test this muscle separately, in isolation from other muscles. The patient resists by attempting to move the arm in the directions, anteriorly, posteriorly and laterally against the practitioner's resistance.

All diagnoses, neurological and orthopaedic muscle testing and medical testing procedures are most important in determining a patient's condition.

This other form of muscle testing as an aid to diagnosis checks a different aspect of mind-brain-body function—that is, the body's electromagnetic life force energy circuitry flow to assess the body's overall condition. It is complementary to neurological and orthopaedic testing and has been tested in parallel to confirm its validity.

Surrogate testing

There can often be times when it is not possible to muscle test a person. This includes cases such as babies or young children, patients who are too weak to be tested, or anyone who is unconscious or asleep. In these situations, an extra person can be used as a surrogate tester.

The practitioner engages the surrogate tester whose life force electromagnetic energy circuitry is linked to the person being tested. This testing is demonstrated and explained during our VET presentations and demonstrations.

Far-reaching discoveries

There have been many far-reaching new discoveries regarding the mind-brain-body with its many levels of functioning extending way beyond the relevance of this book, which is, as you know, the teaching of beneficial self-help techniques. This information can be presented in our workshop programs for anyone who is interested or involved in various fields of research.

There is a mind-brain-body level that is the body's control centre. At this level, we are also able to switch into further levels connected to every part of the body. And then information can be accessed about the vertebral column, spinal cord, sacrum, coccyx and the sacral and coccygeal nerves.

Perhaps accessing information and making corrections, especially at these levels, might seem complicated, but it is a procedure that can be taught and easily understood. It is not difficult or time consuming. In fact, it takes much less time. The mind-brain-body functions as a marvellous biological computer and it functions with precision. It is amazing to observe the immediate overall corrections resulting with the whole body.

The VET program is concerned with the neurological, musculoskeletal integrity of the whole body. Achieving a balanced, erect, relaxed, and neutral posture is of paramount importance. This is explained later in chapter 6, "Posture Balancing and Coordinated Movement." Although the self-help techniques bring body function to a high level of efficiency, it can be greatly enhanced by making corrections at the body's control centre level. So before commencing posture balancing, it is well worthwhile to check and make corrections at this control centre level to ensure all corrections in the body have been made. These corrections are part of our workshop presentation sessions. Guidance with qualified instruction is necessary for this higher level.

A most common detrimental factor with everyone being tested for the first time is to find impairment of the sacral and coccygeal nerves, and there are also detrimental effects along the whole spinal column, spinal cord, and the entire body.

Partial impairment of the sacral and coccygeal nerves

This is a most important far-reaching discovery because of the predisposed detrimental effects with the wide distribution of the sacral and coccygeal nerves within the pelvic girdle, the surrounding musculature, muscles in the legs, and the overall adverse effects on the whole body. In testing this region, my thoughts for this impingement of the sacral nerves is that adhesions have been formed with each nerve as it exits its foramina.

What is the cause of these adhesions? It could have happened initially during that period in the early formative years, from crawling to the upright posture and walking. How often do babies, when attempting to stand upright, fall backwards and sit on the floor? Then of course there are always the possibilities of falls during one's life, perhaps often severe. A sedentary lifestyle or riding a horse or bike could all contribute to causing adhesions. For everyone's benefit, here is some important information about the sacrum, that large triangular-shaped bone at the base of the spine. At birth, the sacrum is comprised of five separate bones joined together by their centres of ossification.

Throughout the years to maturity, these bones fuse together to become one solid bone in adult life. Trauma to these separate bones could also contribute to some degree to this overall impairment of the sacral nerves. As a result of any trauma to this region caused by falls, it is most likely to cause injury and detrimental effects to the coccyx (tail bone), that small bone at the base of the spinal column. The coccyx anchors the spinal cord and is attached by a long slender filament that forms the end of the spinal cord, the *filum terminale*. Any injury to this region can cause tension along the whole length of the spinal cord.

The impact of any falls reverberates along the whole spinal column. It has been exciting to discover how to access information about the effects of trauma to the spinal cord and spinal column, then furthermore to use techniques to restore energy flow to these regions.

This has been a recent discovery. I believe that it opens the doorway to many far-reaching new discoveries.

The multitude of problems and diseases that can develop within and surrounding the pelvic basin are numerous. Because of the wide distribution of the sacral nerves, which emerge through each foramina of the sacrum, the adverse consequences can extend around the whole body. Discovering how common these adverse effects are, and then developing simple techniques to correct and eliminate these detrimental factors, has been a most important development in this research program. The immediate beneficial results become obvious by witnessing the marked improvement that occurs with testing the neurological, musculoskeletal, and functioning aspects of the body.

For example, pain can often be elicited with palpation of the gluteal and other muscles of the pelvic girdle. After using this sacral technique, the pain subsides. Furthermore, it is found that many muscles in the body are not functioning in coordination, which indicates the extent or these adverse effects throughout the body. And most importantly, interference with the sacral nerves can also detrimentally influence the functional physiology within the pelvic basin. Again, the VET techniques activate the neural pathways to correct and restore the overall coordination and synchronization of muscular function in the body. The importance and beneficial effects of fully activating sacral and coccygeal nerve function can be readily appreciated.

Allan Warrener

Communicating with the mind-brain-body by muscle testing and with thought

As you are aware, the mind-brain-body is multidimensional, functioning at many levels or frequencies above the physical level. Muscle testing, when used as an aid to diagnosis, enables us to communicate with the mind-brain-body, our wonderful biological computer. Any dysfunctional points on the body will cause an indicator testing muscle to weaken, thereby providing information about the body. Testing in this manner is going beyond the level of conscious thought to every level of our beings, enabling us to communicate with every level in the higher levels of consciousness—our innate intelligence controlling the whole mind-brain-body. It can also be demonstrated how it is possible to communicate precisely by thought. It is the communication between the higher levels of consciousness. With presentations and demonstrations, the usual procedure is to first check the physical level and then the emotional, mental, causal, and the mind-brain-body control centre levels.

Chapter 5

Balance and Revitalize Your Body

With harmonious breathing, the mind-brain-body functions as an integrated whole unit comprised of a series of bodily systems designed to function in synchronization.

Self-help breathing techniques

Could this be a turning point in our program, where the ancient knowledge of the East merges with the neurological, musculoskeletal, and anatomical aspects of Western science? No longer is there any mention of the chakras, energy channels, or the meridian system. With breathing, our focus is on the neurological and musculoskeletal aspects of the body, the spine, the nervous system, the nerve plexuses, and the endocrine system.

The knowledge that has come from Eastern studies still remains as forming part of the basis, structure, and circuitry of Vortex Energy Therapy. It has only been because of this knowledge that it has been possible to develop this program. The vortexes play an important role with corrections.

Remember, as has already been mentioned, that it can be demonstrated how a simple yet powerful breathing technique immediately corrects and removes common detrimental factors, increases overall strength, and at the same time aligns the whole muscular and skeletal structure. How does this happen?

The mind-brain-body functions as an integrated whole unit that is comprised of a series of systems designed to function in synchronization.

The lungs are part of the respiratory system and function in combination with all other bodily systems; the circulatory system, nervous system, genitourinary system, endocrine system, muscular system, and so forth, all function together in combination with other systems as integral parts of a complete whole unit.

Breathing is usually automatic and subconsciously controlled by the nervous system, the respiratory centre at the base of the brain. The brain and sensory organs in the aorta and carotid arteries sense when the oxygen levels are too low or the carbon dioxide levels are too high. The brain then increases the rate and depth of breathing. This is known as the carbon dioxide reflex. Conversely, when the carbon dioxide levels become low in the bloodstream, breathing is slowed. So the overall body function of this automatic regulatory mechanism involves the respiratory system, nervous system, circulatory system, and muscular system, in combination with other systems functioning in response to the demands or bodily requirements placed on the respiratory system, in particular from muscular exertion.

How do Vortex Energy breathing techniques differ from other forms of breathing exercises?

Understanding the difference is the most important aspect of how the body has been designed to function with breathing in synchronization and in harmony with all the other bodily systems. My experiences, when testing other methods, forms, and types of breathing exercises, has usually been to find that with the breathing exercises, the whole focus is on the lungs in isolation, having the purpose of increasing lung capacity. This approach immediately causes overall dysfunctional effects in the body, with all bodily systems not functioning in synchronization. In contrast to this, with the VET techniques, there is no conscious effort made to breathe, except to blend the breathing exercise in with the automatic rhythm of the breathing.

Movements have been designed to cause the ribcage to expand, with the result that the air comes in and out automatically with inspiration and expiration. Movement occurs along the spinal column. This breathing can be quite subtle and not be able to be perceived, yet it will immediately produce overall beneficial effects in the body. These breathing techniques, which cause movement along the whole spinal column, stimulate all the nerve plexuses and in turn activate all the muscles of inspiration and expiration. Furthermore, this movement along the whole spine markedly increases lung capacity. The objectives are increased lung capacity with breathing automatically and effortlessly.

Learning the self-help breathing techniques

After waking each morning and attending to your daily routine, this is an ideal time to do your breathing techniques while resting on your back. It will stimulate your whole body and cause you to feel refreshed. Of course, any time of day or night is also worthwhile and certainly beneficial. It should be an enjoyable experience anytime. It becomes a part of your daily routine. Any breathing techniques only take a few seconds of your time. Here is a suggestion if you decide to do some breathing techniques on waking each day.

Basic VET breathing

Preparation	Commence your breathing in bed with relaxation. You can also sit on the side of the bed in an upright position. Close your eyes and focus on relaxing your body. Allow your breathing to happen automatically and then perceive the air as it comes through your nostrils. Observe and feel the rhythm of your breathing, how your chest rises and falls with inhalation and exhalation. If you feel any discomfort, then change to a more comfortable position. You are now most likely feeling more relaxed because you are breathing automatically and communicating with your wonderful mind-brain-body.
Technique	To commence the first breathing technique, observe the rhythm of your breathing. As you are about to breathe in automatically, arch your lower back so that it lifts up from the bed. This movement will cause the pelvis to tilt at the same time. Then as you exhale flatten your lower back on the bed and this will cause the pubic region of the pelvis to lift upwards.

Beneficial Effects	As mentioned previously, this breathing technique will produce immediate and overall beneficial effects.

My thoughts for these beneficial effects happening are that the movement of the lower back and pelvis immediately causes the involvement of all bodily systems. The respiratory system immediately commences to function in synchronization with all other bodily systems (the neurological, musculoskeletal, endocrine, and all other bodily systems). The movement along the spine stretches the dura mater, which is the outer membrane covering the spinal cord and brain. This stretching of the dura mater in turn activates the nerve plexuses, the endocrine system, and all other bodily systems.

This breathing technique also activates the neural pathways for this position of lying on your back and feeling more comfortable in this position. Similarly with other positions, the neural pathways for resting on your right side, left side, and face down (prone position) can all be activated by arching your lower back as you breathe in and then curling the pelvis forward as you breathe out. Activating the neural pathways for these different positions will assist in making you feel more comfortable in these positions.

Activating the neural pathways for the intercostal muscles and all the muscles involved with inspiration and expiration to achieve one's maximal lung capacity

When testing anyone, including athletes, for the first time, it is evident that the intercostal muscles and the other muscles involved in breathing are not functioning to assist with breathing. Here is the exercise to activate the neural pathways for these muscles. The second breathing technique can be performed while standing, although it will produce the same therapeutic effects in any position.

Upper chest breathing

Preparation	This technique can be practised and applied any time of the day. It is quite subtle and can be performed at any time without anyone being aware that you are doing your breathing exercise. To maximise the benefits, ensure that you stand straight with your feet shoulder width apart. Relax your body and ensure you are comfortable.
Technique	While sitting, standing, and breathing automatically without any effort, as you are about to inhale, lift your shoulders and roll the shoulders backwards and push your elbows backwards as if you are trying to put your elbows together behind you and then just completely relax your shoulders, with the upper body allowing the exhalation to happen automatically. All movements are performed with ease and relaxation. You might like to add another similar breathing exercise: to lift and roll the shoulders forward with inhalation and then relax and let the air be expelled automatically with exhalation. Although corrections have been made initially with the exercise of the backwards rolling of the shoulders, you can then be reassured that you have balanced the whole body anteriorly and posteriorly.
Beneficial Effects.	The VET breathing techniques immediately restore function and produce beneficial results with increased lung capacity.

With the VET breathing techniques, the breathing happens without effort. It is the overall movement that causes the lung space to expand so that the air enters the expanded lung space. As you lift and roll the shoulders backwards, you will feel your upper chest expand. This exercise will increase the upper lung capacity, and gradually your breathing will come automatically and naturally into this upper region of the lungs.

This exercise can be performed with arms bent at the elbows and hands resting lightly on the upper chest. As your hands lift up to the upper chest while you are lifting and rolling your shoulders backwards, you can feel the expansion of your upper chest and lungs. Or, if you prefer, this exercise can be performed with the arms straight and relaxed.

Breathing exercises to correct muscular imbalance when sitting and standing

It is most common to find that there are overall muscular imbalances in the sitting and standing postures. Although it may not be apparent, these imbalances become evident with testing, especially with the anterior and posterior muscles, and they most likely have been present since early childhood. Simple breathing techniques correct these imbalances, resulting in a relaxed, balanced posture.

The breathing techniques are performed in different positions, while in bed, on the couch, sitting in a chair, or standing. The above-mentioned exercises are not time consuming and can become a part of your daily routine whenever you prefer.

Summary of breathing techniques

The VET breathing techniques have been developed to blend with overall body function, with the movement causing the lungs to expand, resulting in the air automatically flowing into the expanded space. In contrast, many deep breathing exercises and practices consciously focus mainly on inhaling to get as much air as possible through the nostrils, with focus on the lungs in isolation to increase capacity. Although this approach can produce beneficial results and increase lung capacity, this form of breathing is not in synchronization and causes overall imbalances in the body. It is excessively out of proportion with the overall requirements of the body.

It is most important to draw awareness that with divers or underwater swimmers, it is a dangerous practice to hyperventilate to increase the oxygen levels in the bloodstream and to then hold their breaths, for the rapid decrease with oxygen in the blood can cause fainting underwater. Because of the excess of oxygen in the bloodstream, the carbon dioxide neurological reflex is not registering, and consequently the diver can suddenly lose consciousness. Remember, the body is comprised of a series of systems designed to function in synchronization with all other bodily systems as an integrated whole unit.

With the VET program, it is important to remember that with inhalation and exhalation in making corrections, the mouth should always remain closed.

Breathing in the sitting position is explained in chapter 6, "Posture Balancing and Coordinated Movement," because it is a breathing technique to correct posture in the sitting position by activating the neural pathways for good posture. It is an excellent exercise that you can do at any time while sitting at your desk or a table. Just take two or three breaths whenever you would like to refresh yourself.

Chapter 6

Posture Balancing and Coordinated Movement

Our main focus and the central part and aim of this program is to ensure that the whole muscular and skeletal structure is balanced and that the body is coordinated and functioning in synchronization with all movements. Apart from balancing the body on the treatment table, posture balance changes are important in the sitting and erect postures.

All aspects of the Vortex Energy Therapy (VET) program are important. Presentations and demonstrations make it easier to understand what is happening along the way because they provide the opportunities to quickly explain any important features while demonstrating so that any particular aspect can be observed to be actually happening. As anyone advances with the knowledge and expertise of the whole system, it can be appreciated how corrections quickly bring the mind-brain-body to function with maximal efficiency.

Techniques to correct and acquire relaxed, balanced, and erect posture with coordinated movement sequence patterns have been exciting discoveries with this research program, playing a major role in becoming capable of performing at one's potential. An exhilarating discovery with these techniques is being able to activate the neural pathways for any posture or for a variety of movement sequences, such as with the learning of new skills. With the muscular imbalances in the body usually present since the formative years, it is difficult for anyone to develop relaxed, balanced, and erect posture. Being able to activate the neural pathways for ideal posture will facilitate its development. With testing, the immediate changes become evident after correction.

It is usually found with most people that their postures have changed through their lives to adapt to circumstances, work, injuries, habits, and so forth, from the formative years. It would be very difficult for them to alter their postures from one which might seem to be a comfortable position into one that requires a conscious effort to hold and is not easy to maintain. Some coaches might instruct their athletes to keep the tail in, tummy in, chest out, and stand tall, but trying to maintain this posture causes overall muscular tension.

Aligning the structure

The correct pelvic tilt and alignment of the head, neck, and cervical spine provides the basis for good posture, ensuring that the centre of gravity line from the top of the skull falls through the weight-bearing joints of the lower back, lumbar spine, and hip joints and then is aligned parallel to the femur and tibia bones. Perhaps this sounds like a simple way of describing good posture, and that is all that is intended. Remember that muscles move bones, so it is the overall balance of the musculature that balances and aligns the skeletal structure. But then, as you would realize, there are many factors that can and do cause muscular imbalances. It might seem like a complicated procedure to align the structure, balance the musculature, and correct and eliminate the adverse effects of stress, common detrimental factors, and faulty habits that have developed through the years.

Good posture can be demonstrated. With good posture, when standing with a relaxed, balanced, erect, neutral posture, breathing more deeply into the upper chest causes the centre of gravity line to move forward, and this will result in gravity lifting me onto my toes. If I exhale more than normal, gravity causes me to fall backwards.

Here is why this VET program is exciting. In one session of approximately an hour, these adverse and detrimental factors can be corrected and eliminated with simple self-help techniques. This can be demonstrated and explained. The changes with relaxed, erect posture and movements cause immediate testable results.

In early childhood, with the development from crawling to the erect posture and walking, it is a period of learning new skills involving an innumerable variety of movement sequences and habits. These habits become submerged in the subconscious mind, activating neural pathways for a wide variety of movement sequences. With all movements, there is a movement sequence pattern involving the facilitation and inhibition of numerous muscles within each phase of the movement. When one muscle (the agonist) contracts, its opposite or opposing muscle (the antagonist) relaxes because of an automatic neural reflex action. At the same time, other muscles throughout the body act in a synergic manner to support the structure and the muscles of posture.

It has been found with testing through the years that overall muscular imbalances develop as a result of many common detrimental factors and various traumas. The body adapts to a posture that is comfortable for the person.

It is most important that posture is checked and corrected in different positions when sitting and standing to ensure that the body is coordinated and balanced with movement.

Posture in the sitting position

When testing anyone for the first time in the sitting position, it is found that the neural pathways for this position have not been activated, even though the neural pathways for the erect posture have already been activated. So if anyone attempts to sit upright for a period of time, it is not comfortable and becomes tiring for that person. Here is the breathing technique for anyone to correct the neural pathways for sitting. This breathing technique should become part of your daily routine. Just two or three breaths are well worthwhile anytime you are seated.

Seated breathing technique

| Preparation | Incorporate the VET breathing technique while seated as a part of your daily routine.

Sit as tall as you can at the edge of your chair, with your knees bent at right angles, feet flat on the floor and the palms of your hands on your knees. In sitting tall, avoid tilting the chin upwards. During inhalation, the chin remains parallel to the floor. The mouth remains closed all the time with all Vortex Energy breathing techniques. You don't try to breathe in but just let it happen with the rhythm of your breathing. |
|---|---|
| Technique | As you feel you are about to inhale, let your body move forward as you inhale, with your back straight, and keep inhaling as you move backwards, with your back still remaining straight. Then relax completely as you exhale. Remember to not tilt the chin up or down. It can relax at the conclusion of the movement.

The breathing rhythm with most people is two seconds of inhalation and two seconds of exhalation, so the rhythm that would be comfortable would be a one-second inhalation when moving the torso forward and continuing with this inhalation for another second while moving backwards.

For others who breathe more deeply, a four-second inhalation breath might be more suitable. That is, an inhalation of two seconds with the torso moving forward and two seconds while moving backwards. Try to move and breathe with the natural rhythm of your breathing. At the end of each inhalation let your body completely relax allowing the air to be expelled effortlessly. |

In summary, the musculature can be balanced and coordinated on the treatment table and demonstrated as being corrected with everyone. But then the body's overall balance needs to be checked and corrected with sitting, standing, and movement. It is again necessary to activate the neural pathways for these postures and movements. This neural pathway activation can be accomplished in all these situations with simple self-help breathing techniques

Walking requires another type of self-help technique, which is explained in chapter 7, "The Body in Motion." This simple self-help technique is the arm-swinging exercise, which coordinates and synchronizes the joints of the arms and legs, particularly to ensure that the wrists and ankles are moving in synchronization at the same rates. One's focus is placed on the movement of the whole arms from the shoulder joints and also at the wrist joints, at the same time feeling the harmonious tendency of movements at the ankle joints and legs.

Chapter 7

The Body in Motion—Walking, Running, Playing Sports, and Other Activities

It is most important to test the overall condition of the body after walking, running, sports, or any other activities. Although muscular imbalances have been corrected on the treatment table and the sitting and standing positions, it is usually found with testing that the overall muscular function is uncoordinated and not balanced with movement. The arm and leg movements are not coordinated; the movements at the joints are not functioning in synchronization.

As mentioned previously, a major factor with physical development in the formative years is from crawling to the upright posture and walking, which involves the activation of neural pathways for a wide variety of movement sequence patterns with the learning of new skills. Faulty habits are often formed during this period and carried throughout the years. These imbalances, which become evident after walking or movement, can be demonstrated with explanations and corrected on the treatment table and also while seated, standing, and walking.

Viewing the body from a different perspective and explaining the locations of three corresponding sets of vortexes on the body

If the body is viewed from a different perspective as being balanced on all fours, hands and feet, it can be more easily perceived how the shoulders correspond with the hips, elbows with knees, forearms with calves, wrists with ankles, and hands with feet.

On the body there are three main sets of vortexes. One set is on the torso (V), the second set on the legs (VL) and the third set on the arms (VA).

The first set on the torso (V) commences with the first vortex in the coccygeal region. The second vortex is in the pubic region (ovaries, testes), the third vortex in the diaphragm. The fourth vortex is in the mid chest. The fifth vortex is in the throat.

With the second set of vortexes (VL) the first vortex is in the feet, the second the ankles, the third the calves, the fourth the knees and the fifth the hip joints.

The third set of vortexes is on the arms (VA). The first vortex Is in the hands, the second the wrists, the third the forearms, the fourth the elbows, and the fifth the shoulders.

With all three sets the sixth and seventh vortexes remain the same, the centre of the forehead and the crown as these are higher intuition and spiritual centres.

First Vortex	Hands, feet, and coccygeal region
Second Vortex	Wrists, ankles, and pubic region

Third Vortex	Diaphragm, forearms, and calves
Fourth Vortex	Mid chest, elbows, and knees
Fifth Vortex	Throat, shoulders, and hips

Referring to this chart with the location of the vortexes, you will notice that the vortexes at these corresponding joints are the same vortexes. For example, the fifth vortexes are at the shoulders, hips and throat. The fourth vortexes are at the elbows, knee joints, and the centre of the chest. The third vortexes are at the forearms, lower legs, and diaphragmatic region. The second vortexes are at the wrists, ankles, and pubic region, and then there are the first vortexes, at the hands, feet, and the coccygeal region. For the body to function in coordination with synchronization of movement at corresponding joints, the corresponding vortexes should spin or spiral at the same rates or frequencies, but when testing anyone for the first time, this spinning is not in synchronization, so it is not possible for this person to function with maximal efficiency.

An analogy that could be used to explain this is that if you imagine a strong coil spring at one knee joint and a weaker coil spring at the other knee, then it immediately becomes obvious how the whole body is thrown out of balance. Using the VET techniques is similar to replacing all springs with springs of equal strength at corresponding joints, shoulders and hips, elbows and knees, forearms and calves, wrists and ankles, and hands and feet to restore overall balance, coordination, and synchronization with movement.

Perhaps we could take our imaginations a little further and visualize the spiralling of a vortex. It is easy to imagine the shape of a vortex as a coiled spring. Then imagine if we had a coil spring under each foot and another under each heel and ankle. What expectations would we have if we ran with these coiled springs under our feet and ankles? We would want to feel the bouncing action of these springs, wouldn't we? The spring in our steps is the main focus and objective with the body in motion, and this can be achieved with the following exercise to ensure that all of the corresponding joints are functioning in synchronization, especially the wrists and ankles. That is the purpose of the rhythmical arm-swinging exercises.

My reason for presenting the analogy of coiled springs at joints is to develop awareness of our overall aim and the importance for all corresponding joints to function in synchronization to achieve maximal efficiency with movement. For balance to be achieved, both the joints and the muscles need to function harmoniously and in synchronization. This the reason for VET arm swinging techniques to accomplish the overall balance and synchronization.

Arm-swinging exercises, initially using paper drumsticks, having awareness and focus of the movements at the wrists causing the rhythmical feeling of movement at the ankles

Paper drumsticks are recommended for safety, just in case a lightly held wooden drum sticks should slip from one's hands. For this you can roll your own drum sticks from two large sheets of paper and then discard them when you have experienced the overall rhythmical balance with movement in the body.

Allan Warrener

Preparation	Find a suitable location with ample space both in front of you, behind you, and also to your left and right sides.
Technique	The purpose of holding a drumstick in each hand is to focus on the movement at each wrist. Then swing each arm alternatively, as you would if you were running. Imagine that there is a sloping drum in front of you at approximately waist level and then alternately hit the "drum" with left and right drumsticks. The focus is on the wrist joints hitting the drum as well as the whole arm from the shoulder joints. The objective is also to feel a slight movement in each ankle and foot, to develop and feel the overall rhythmical movement of the body. As each arm swings through, it straightens and relaxes at the completion of each swing. Each arm will rebound back to bend automatically at the elbow no more than ninety degrees so that it does not bend too much. As each arm rebounds back and bends at the elbow, the hands should not come up higher than shoulder level, as this is a wasted movement. There should not be any effort made to lift the arm back; it should rebound automatically and be relaxed.
Beneficial Effects	Relaxed, rhythmical arm-swinging exercises combined with other techniques synchronize these rates of spinning with the corresponding vortexes and ensure that overall balance with movement is restored and maintained. The immediate relaxed ease of movement with balance, felt with walking, often brings with it feelings of exhilaration and well-being. The immediate changes are quite obvious. Because of the overall integrated movements, the balance and coordination also results in conserving energy while walking.

The alignment of posture can be varied with these arm-swinging exercises and is especially valuable for athletes who would like to improve their forward body lean and speed with sprinting. The aim of this exercise is to achieve overall balance and coordination. You will appreciate this happening when you experience the feeling of movement in the feet and ankles as well as the hands and wrists.

When walking after this exercise, the arms should just hang in a relaxed fashion and move automatically in tempo with the walking pace. In walking at a faster pace, the relaxed arms swing automatically at a faster tempo. When the body is balanced in this way, it will function in balance even with carrying objects of different weights in each hand or having to avoid obstacles or uneven terrain while walking. The overall balance will be retained.

Dancing in time with the music

With most sports and activities such as ballroom dancing, a change of pace, speed, or tempo usually causes overall muscular imbalances in the body. These variations in tempo tests have been conducted with music, using a metronome, or often just handclapping. The VET techniques correct any adverse effects when adapting to any changes in timing to ensure that balance, coordination and rhythm are maintained. This is most important and worthwhile to check as a part of the program. Remember in chapter 2 the story about Volodymyr Kuts and his surging tactics in winning the 10,000 metres at the 1956 Olympic Games in Melbourne.

Techniques to facilitate the learning of new skills

With the learning of any new skills for sports or any other activities, learning to play the piano or any musical instruments, new dance routines, touch typing, and so on, the main aim is to reach the stage when the movements are performed automatically, with only a minimum of conscious thought. The techniques, which activate neural pathways for a variety of movement sequence patterns for the new skills, are used in combination with practice and visualization to mentally imprint the movement, which is practised so that it eventually becomes automatic. This is explained in detail in chapter 16.

With regard to learning new skills, it is also worthwhile to remember that in chapter 2, it is explained how important it is to ensure that the neural pathways are activated for the movement from resting in bed to sitting on the side of the bed and then standing. Otherwise, there is an overall weakening and muscular imbalance of the body, resulting in the person having to pause for a moment to feel balanced before moving.

To activate the neural pathways for these movements, the person performs the movement that goes from resting in bed or on the couch to the sitting position on the side of the bed or couch and then standing and walking a few steps. Then any VET self-help breathing technique will activate the neural pathways for these movements after they have been performed.

I would suggest the following exercise while standing: roll your shoulders up and backwards, also pressing both elbows backwards as you inhale and then relax your body and allow the lungs to exhale automatically. Remember, it is the movement that causes expansion of the lungs, with the air coming effortlessly into the expanded space.

Instead of discussing vortexes and using the analogy of coiled springs, let's talk about how overall muscular imbalances can occur because of a neurological dysfunction that I have found with testing is a most common detrimental factor.

Allan Warrener competing in a half-mile event

Photo courtesy of a friend

As mentioned in this chapter, using the analogy of a strong coiled spring at one knee joint and a weaker coiled spring at the other knee, overall imbalance results. VET self-help arm-swinging techniques correct all imbalances. It would be difficult for any athlete, sports person, or anyone to overcome these imbalances, whereas the Vortex Energy Therapy techniques immediately make the corrections. Another pleasing feature is that this conserves energy with walking, running, and all movements.

In Chapter 13 it is more fully explained how there is a common neurological dysfunction with the timing mechanism between the contraction of the agonist muscles (facilitation) and the relaxation of the opposite antagonist muscles (inhibition).

Let us now think only about the nervous system and focus on the contraction and relaxation of muscles. When there is overall imbalance with the musculature, it has been found with our testing that there is a neurological timing delay between the facilitation and inhibition of approximately three to four seconds, which is the inhibitory nerve impulses acting on the opposite antagonist muscles.

At this stage, when making corrections, the Vortex Energy Therapy rhythmical arm-swinging techniques are coordinating and synchronizing the overall musculature of the body by influencing the neuromuscular spindles and Golgi tendon organs. It is important with this technique that the focus is on the relaxed arm, wrist, and shoulder movements and to then feel both ankles and feet moving rhythmically in coordination with the wrists and hands, as explained in this chapter.

With using the correct relaxed, rhythmical arm-swinging technique, the coordinated movement can be felt in both feet. It can then be appreciated that the mind-brain-body is functioning as an integrated whole unit involving the nervous system and functioning in combination and synchronization with all other bodily systems.

You can use this gentle arm-swinging exercise anytime, standing balanced with your feet slightly and comfortably apart. Remember, the arm swinging is relaxed and not strenuous.

Again, another important point is to try not to consciously swing your arms when walking; let the arms just hang relaxed and move freely. For example, if you are walking and suddenly turn around, just let the arms hang loose and even fly around away from the body.

You will now, of course, realize that we are only talking about the neurological and musculoskeletal aspects of the body with movement, without any mention of the vortexes, but often it has been though the ancient knowledge of the East that so many wonderful discoveries have been made, tested in combination and in parallel and correlated with the neurological and musculoskeletal aspects of the body to gradually culminate in this therapeutic program.

Chapter 8

A Guided Relaxation, Personal Development, Goal-Setting Visualization Session

Nothing truly valuable arises from ambition or from a mere sense of duty; it stems rather from love and devotion toward men and toward objective things.

—Albert Einstein

Feelings are an integral part of mind-brain-body function. The beautiful feelings of love and gratitude are produced with the life force energy that comes through the fourth vortex. Feelings of comfort and security are produced, with the life force energy coming through the first vortex. Feelings of sensual pleasure of all the senses come with the life force energy through the second vortex, while feelings of control enter through the third vortex. Then of paramount importance are the feelings of expression. There is an energy which enters the body through the fifth vortex. This is the energy which enables us to express our feelings and to experience the feelings of fulfilment and well-being.

Suggestions for a guided relaxation, revitalization, personal development, and goal-setting visualization session

Let's now enjoy a re-energizing, revitalizing session of relaxation. Here are some suggestions to help you relax. Remember that your mind-brain-body functions as a marvellous biological computer. We are now beginning to set the program for all that we are planning to achieve. Here are some thoughts about being able to go into a state of relaxation just like turning off a switch.

Preparation	We commence by just letting the whole body completely relax. We also want to ensure, if it is cold, that we are covered to keep warm and feel comfortable while lying flat on our backs. We think, *I am enjoying relaxing my whole body.*
Technique	First we perceive our breathing. We just let the breath happen by itself, focusing on the air coming through our nostrils as it enters the body and perceiving the breath as it comes in and out through our nostrils. And we think, *I am letting my whole body relax.* We are not trying to breathe; we just feel the breath, what is happening as it comes into the body, and we feel the rise and fall of the chest. Each time as the chest sinks down, we let the body relax more. *I am letting my whole body relax.* If we feel uncomfortable anywhere, we just make ourselves more comfortable and keep feeling the breathing as it happens automatically. Gradually, each time we breathe out, we just let the body sink more into a beautiful state of being relaxed. We keep on thinking, *I am letting my whole body relax.*

> Then we take our awareness into feeling the body, feeling the feet from within. We feel the right foot and remain focused on the right foot for a few seconds—then feel the left foot and remain focused on the left foot for a few seconds.
>
> We completely relax the right leg and then completely relax the left leg. Then we relax the whole of the pelvis. As we breathe out, we feel the spine flatten on the floor and relax. The right arm is relaxed, as are the hand and fingers. We relax the left arm, hand, and fingers. We relax the face, smiling and thinking how pleasant it is to relax.

Feelings that are an integral part of mind-body function

Now we will bring energy into the body. We are going to visualise this vital life force energy coming into the body through a series of vortexes in different regions. It is through this series of vortexes that we get the energy with the feelings that are an integral part of mind-brain-body function.

Visualize a beautiful rainbow. We can see the sun shining through the beautiful colours of the rainbow: red, orange, yellow, green, blue, indigo, and violet. Imagine that we are resting under this rainbow. We are going to bring these beautiful sunburst colours with our life force energy into the body.

| **First Vortex**

Colour: Red
Feeling: Security
Musical Note: C | Visualize the beautiful red mist colour of the rainbow with the sun shining through this red mist. It enters the body through the vortexes in the feet, in both hands, and through the base of the spine in the region of the coccyx bone. This is the energy that produces within us the feelings of being comfortable and secure: *I am bringing in the energy. I am breathing in the energy to ensure that I am feeling calm, comfortable, confident and secure.*

This energy has a frequency that corresponds to the musical note C. We can activate this vortex by playing this musical note or by holding a red cloth or paper over one of the first vortexes. Of course, all vortexes can be activated with the energy from the hand of the practitioner or with the self-help breathing techniques.

It is interesting how these feelings of being comfortable and secure are associated with these regions of the body, the hands, feet, and base of the spine. Imagine that you are riding a horse and think about what you feel most. As you are riding this horse, you are feeling that your feet are fastened firmly in the stirrups, that you have a strong grip on the reins, and that you are comfortably seated in the saddle. |

Second Vortex Colour: Orange Feelings: our sensual enjoyment and pleasure through touch, taste, sounds, sight, and smell Musical note: D	Then we see the beautiful orange mist of the rainbow with the sun shining through. The energy in the orange mist enters the body through the vortexes in the pubic region, through the ovaries in women and testes in men, and through the vortexes in both the wrists and ankles. *I am breathing in the energy to produce pleasant or pleasurable feelings of all the senses.* This vortex can be activated by playing the musical note D. It can also be activated by holding the colour orange over one of these second vortexes.
Third Vortex Colour: Yellow Feelings: Conscious and subconscious control Musical Note: E	The next energy is the beautiful sunburst yellow. This energy comes through the vortexes in the diaphragmatic region, the lower legs, and both forearms. *I am breathing in the energy to ensure that I am in control at all times in all situations.* This energy can be activated by playing the musical note E or by placing a yellow cloth or paper over the third vortex.
Fourth Vortex Colour: Green Feelings: love and gratitude Musical Note: F	Green is everywhere in nature. The view from our windows might be truly beautiful and uplifting, with green grass, trees, bushes, and shrubs. And then there is the beautiful sunny green mist of the rainbow. Just visualize this beautiful green energy. *I am grateful to be able to breathe in the energy to develop my feelings of love, gratitude, kindness, appreciation, caring, concern, and compassion.*

	We see this energy vortex spiralling into the body through the centre of the chest, through both elbows, and through both knees. Again this energy overlaps the pelvic region. Then we visualize another green vortex just above the head, with energy cascading down over the entire body. The musical note F or the colour green activates the fourth vortex.
Fifth Vortex Colour: Blue Feeling: Expression and fulfilment Musical Note: G	With all of these feelings—comfort, security, sensuality, control, love, and gratitude—we need a specific energy for each feeling to produce these feelings, which play an integral role in mind-brain-body function. But then of paramount importance, we need another type of energy to enable us to express these feelings, to experience a feeling of fulfilment, to feel happiness or satisfaction by fully achieving our potential. It is a beautiful blue energy that enables us to experience this level of fulfilment, the wonderful feeling of well-being. Just visualize the sun shining through this beautiful blue mist of the rainbow. *I am breathing in the energy to enable me to express my feelings, that I may know and love and serve, also helping others in whatever way I can.* This energy enters the body through the vortexes in the throat and both shoulders, and it overlaps the whole torso, from the pubic region to the neck. This is the energy that enables us to express our feelings and experience fulfilment of our feelings. So we are going to relax completely, observe the breathing, and let this revitalizing energy flow into our bodies. This energy is to ensure that we are calm, confident, comfortable, and secure, that there is enjoyment and pleasure in our lives, that we are in control at all times and experiencing the wonderful feelings of love and gratitude, kindness, care, concern and compassion.

Personal development and goal-setting visualization

Now while we are feeling completely relaxed in this pleasant state of being, the alpha state, we can visualize ourselves achieving any goals that we would like to accomplish. Perhaps you would like to lose weight and enjoy better health. Then see yourself as you would like to be. You might even say, "I am strong, healthy, energetic, enthusiastic, and enjoying life while having the physique that I want." Or perhaps you might like to reinforce those feelings and say, "I am feeling calm, comfortable, confident, and secure. I am enjoying the pleasant sensual feelings throughout my whole body. I am in control at all times. I feel grateful for the warm feelings of love and friendship that we all share with each other."

Each one of us is unique. We each have a purpose in life. There are so many goals that we would like to achieve, so now is the time to visualize what you would like to do. See yourself doing it now. What will happen? Your mind-brain-body, your wonderful biological computer, your faithful servant, will guide you subconsciously towards these goals that you would like to achieve. Whatever it may be that you want to achieve, even if you get off course sometimes, it will redirect you back to achieve these goals.

Sometimes you may not realise what you want to achieve, but if you put this thought to your mind-brain-body, it will gradually come up with different thoughts and ideas that will allow you to see much more clearly the direction to take to achieve these goals. It is certainly worthwhile to spend some time in visualizing whatever it is that you would like to accomplish. Just relax for a few minutes to visualise what you want to achieve. See yourself now achieving the goals you would like to become reality. Talk to yourself in the mirror each morning and say, "I like you. You are my friend. Thank you for all you are doing for me!" Whenever you have a glass of water, just think, *With love and gratitude.*

Chapter 9

Stress and Stress Patterns

I am breathing in the energy to ensure that I feel calm, comfortable, confident, secure, in control at all times in every situation, revitalizing with breathing and relaxation.

Stress patterns

When testing anyone for the first time, although it may not be obvious, it is expected to find that there is an overall condition, a phenomenon, that I have termed a stress pattern. With testing, the following factors become evident:

- Overall muscular imbalances, structural misalignments, and uncoordinated movement sequence patterns.
- A pattern of misalignment along the spine, with overall muscular imbalances presenting a false impression of a difference in leg lengths. It is not an actual anatomical difference in each leg but only the appearance that there is, resulting from the overall imbalanced pull of the musculature.

Of course, there can sometimes be an actual anatomical difference as a result of fractures or perhaps with hip replacement surgery, when the surgeon might decide to slightly alter the leg length. Pelvis and spine are adversely affected by stress, with the body becoming susceptible to pain, strains, sprains, and injuries.

- A general weakness of muscles throughout the body in comparison to their potential strength.
- An overall neurological dysfunction causing a delay in timing between the facilitation and inhibition of the agonist and antagonist muscles not switching immediately. This is explained in more detail in Chapter 13, which covers many aspects of sporting injuries.

The point to test for the presence of a stress pattern, as explained in chapter 3, "The Structure of Vortex Energy Therapy," is the heart meridian point at the tip of the little finger. The weakening of an indicator testing muscle confirming a stress pattern will immediately reveal all of the above information about the body. These detrimental factors have been demonstrated countless times. My expectation after corrections have been made is that the corrections and elimination for an overall stress pattern will hold. It is possible, however, that stress can still adversely affect the body in different ways.

But this is the purpose of teaching the Vortex Energy techniques, to develop awareness, to know and understand how this can occur and to ensure that it does not happen. Becoming aware of common thoughts, attitudes, feelings, habits, and emotions is such an important step in developing awareness, helping us to recognize the cause of stressful situations or how stress can develop and how frustrating and futile it can sometimes be to try to communicate with some people because their attitudes act as barriers to communication, learning, development, and well-being. This information is presented in chapter 10, "States of Mind."

The memories of many stressful situations may often remain, but the Vortex Energy Therapy techniques correct and eliminate the discordant and detrimental effects of all stress on the body by restoring function to the affected circuitry. The aim of this whole program is to allow the mind-brain-body to function with maximal efficiency. In achieving this aim, the adverse effects no longer remain.

With initial testing, if you ask that person to think of a few stressful situations, but of course not revealing these cases, a chosen indicator testing muscle will weaken and a stress pattern becomes evident. The memories of stressful situations may have been forgotten, but the adverse effects of stressful situations still remain submerged in the psyche like old programs in our biological computers. If the person is unable to recall any memories of any stressful situation and the practitioner just says words such as anxiety, frustration, grief, doubts, anger, fear, and so forth, an indicator testing muscle will weaken.

Perhaps an easy way to explain the process of how the self-help techniques correct and eliminate the detrimental effects of stress is that the breathing techniques restore function to the body's vital life force, electromagnetic circuitry that has been adversely affected by the stress. As you are aware, the lungs form part of the respiratory system, which functions in combination with all other bodily systems as integral parts of a complete unit, the mind-brain-body, so it can be more easily understood how a single breath can influence the whole body. The respiratory system, functioning in combination with all other systems, responds to the requirements of overall body function in restoring function to any dysfunctional circuitry that has been adversely affected by stress.

How stress affects the body internally and externally

Internal stress can be caused by emotional factors such as anger, anxiety, sadness, grief, fear, sorrow, annoyance, and so forth. These factors are known as the endogenous factors.

There are external or exogenous factors such as extreme changes in weather temperature, airborne pollutants caused by fires, floods, tornadoes, and so forth, carried by winds around the world. There are many different stressful factors causing overall upsets in the body.

Here is the exciting part: once these corrections are made, the body immediately becomes stress-free. The program will guide you how to remain in this state of being. Stress can be physical, emotional, mental, or environmental. That is the body's allergic reaction to different environments.

Stress: physical, mental, emotional, and environmental

The body can be adversely affected environmentally by many external factors. Of course while it is widely acknowledged that stress can detrimentally affect the body in many ways, it can be demonstrated and precisely predicted, with our VET program how stress can adversely affect the neurological and musculoskeletal aspects of body function, which at the same time can detrimentally affect functional physiology and the whole body.

Then furthermore, it becomes evident that the VET techniques correct and eliminate these harmful effects, which are predisposing the body to injuries and illnesses. It becomes evident with testing, that the body immediately functions at a much higher level of efficiency. Whilst the memories of stressful situations might still be recalled, the adverse effects of these past traumas no longer remain.

Stress patterns predispose the body to injuries and illnesses and hinder everyone from performing at his or her potential. Stress patterns in sports, often the reason for lacklustre performances, can be corrected and eliminated with the VET techniques, and this condition can be maintained.

The physical level

There is an overall assessment with corrections and eliminations of many common detrimental factors such as stress patterns developed from early childhood and the formative years. Then there are many other factors, as already mentioned, such as extreme changes in weather temperature, airborne pollutants carried by winds around the world, prostheses and scar tissue causing blockages in energy flow, eye movements causing muscles to weaken, impairment of the sacral and coccygeal nerves, as well as any other factors that need to be corrected.

Self-image

Self-image affects the body differently from the usual stress patterns, in that it involves the body's feelings.

As mentioned previously, one's self-image has been found to be affected by stress, usually at an early age. Again, during any workshops, an opportunity is provided to demonstrate the immediate beneficial effects of breathing and other self-help techniques with corrections and the development of a vibrant new self-image.

Switching from the physical level to the emotional level

After making these corrections at a physical level and testing, it would appear as if no more corrections are needed, but at this stage, the demonstrations become more fascinating in being able to show how the mind-brain-body functions with precision at every level. In switching to an emotional level, stress factors again become evident, strong muscles become weak, and the overall condition of the body changes. But then switching back to the physical level, the body is immediately changed back to the way it was after corrections, with no sign of any stress. Weak muscles become strong again, with the whole body functioning at a high level of efficiency. So it becomes obvious that corrections need to be made at an emotional level, but at this level, it is the different aspects of feelings that can adversely affect the body.

Emotional aspects of feelings

On an emotional level, it can be demonstrated how each of the following aspects of feelings specifically affect different regions on both sides of the body, predisposing the body to illness.

- Stifled or unreciprocated feelings
- Suppressed or unexpressed feelings
- Conflicting thoughts and feelings
- Separation

It is quite amazing how these discoveries eventuated as a result of wondering what the initial cause of a patient's condition was. These emotional aspects can be demonstrated.

Whilst relaxation therapy and meditation are worthwhile, beneficial, and certainly recommended in dealing with the symptoms of stress, these approaches, according to scientific studies, do not remove the causes of stress adversely affecting the body.

The VET techniques are most effective in correcting and eliminating the factors causing any adverse effects in the body. The techniques also restore function to all regions of the body. Although innumerable forms of stress have been tested in this program, it would be inappropriate and of little value to discuss in any detail the many types of stress and lose sight of our objective: *to bring mind-brain-body function to its highest level of efficiency and to become capable of performing at one's potential by using the VET self-help techniques.*

With presentations and demonstrations, much information can be shared about accessing the many levels and assessing the overall conditions of the body, but it is not relevant to the main focus of our Vortex Energy Therapy program, the self-help techniques.

Activating neural pathways by integrating the right and left hemispheres of the brain

Techniques to activate the neural pathways by integrating the right and left hemispheres of the brain are an exciting feature of this program.

Balancing both male and female circuitry to flow in harmony

Within the body, there is both a male and a female circuitry. It can be demonstrated with muscle testing by touching the right and left sides of the body when these circuits are not flowing in harmony. With corrections, it can be demonstrated how both circuitries are flowing in harmony.

Chapter 10

States of Mind

Here are some beautiful thoughts from the meditations of Marcus Aurelius, who was the emperor of Rome from 161 AD for ten years, until his death in 180 AD.

> ***Begin each day by telling yourself: Today I shall be meeting with interference, ingratitude, insolence, disloyalty, ill-will, and selfishness— all of them due to the offenders' ignorance of what is good or evil. But for my part I have long perceived the nature of good and its nobility, the nature of evil and its meanness, and also the nature of the culprit himself, who is my brother (not in the physical sense, but as a fellow creature similarly endowed with reason and a share of the divine), therefore none of those things can injure me, for nobody can implicate me in what is degrading.***

It's a wonderful world we live in! There is nothing wrong with the world. It's some of the people who are the problem. These beautiful thoughts of Marcus Aurelius's could remind us each morning not to become distracted and influenced by negative people. Perhaps we could help to change them but be aware not to become implicated in their negativity.

This first section is about thoughts, feelings, and attitudes while developing awareness. We could begin by asking ourselves what our attitudes are. Are they negative or positive? In our everyday activities, we tend to become creatures of habit. Are these worthwhile habits? If we would like to change, we need to become aware of our thoughts, feeling, attitudes, habits, and emotions. Ask yourself the following questions: Who am I? What is my purpose in life? Is it a worthwhile and worthy purpose? Having a worthy purpose and making a commitment to achieve that purpose is a powerful force that can drive you and keep you focused along your journey. Goals can be set as steps along the way in achieving your purpose.

Becoming aware is so important because these thoughts, attitudes, habits and emotions are shaping our lives and moulding the characters of each of us into the individuals that we become, each with our own unique and distinctive qualities. These thoughts and habits can also adversely affect us, as has been mentioned previously, as being old programs in our biocomputers.

There are four different states of mind, each illustrated with a diagram. This is a most important part of the whole program because of the influence of the attitudes and thoughts on mind-brain-body function.

First illustration —common negative thoughts, attitudes, feelings, and emotions

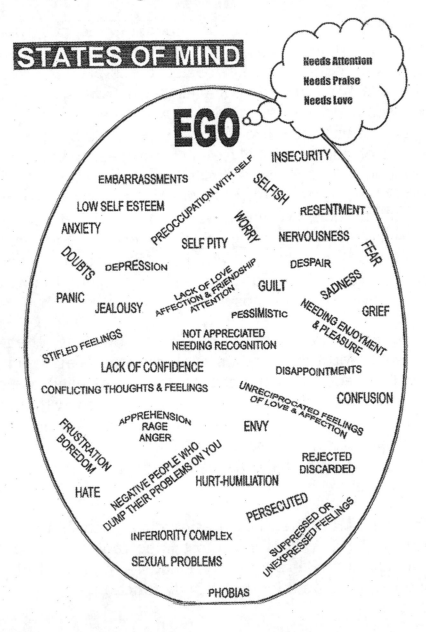

When the mind is cluttered with negative thoughts, attitudes, feelings, and emotions, how much mind space remains clear for thinking clearly or having clarity of thought, and what adverse influence does negative thinking have on the decisions that are made or the directions that are taken? Where did the information listed in the first illustration come from? It eventuated during one of our Vortex Energy workshops, when everyone was asked to contribute with negative thoughts to be written on the whiteboard in order to help develop awareness.

We need to develop awareness of common negative thoughts, attitudes, feelings, and emotions that have developed into habits over periods of many years and have become submerged in the mind, influencing and hindering clarity of thought, causing predisposition to stress, and adversely affecting the body. Here are some examples that are listed in the first illustration: *anxiety, frustration, anger, annoyance, hate, despair, resentment, envy, guilt, insecurity, pessimism, argumentativeness, and so forth.* The detrimental effects of the impact of just saying or reading these words can be demonstrated.

The Vortex Energy Therapy program demonstrates how to correct and eliminate the detrimental effects of any of these negative thoughts, feelings, and emotions. Remember also the powerful effects that can be made by just thinking of saying the words "with love and gratitude." These words will immediately revitalize and energize the whole body.

Second illustration---obstacles to learning, communication, and development

A mind with restricting attitudes and obstacles to learning, communication, and development

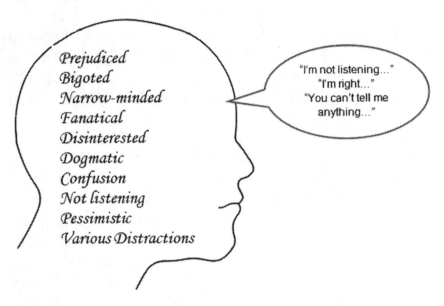

Of course, all of the thoughts, feelings, and attitudes in the first diagram would certainly be a hindrance to learning, communication, and development. In the diagram above, there are barriers to communication, with attitudes such as being prejudiced, narrow-minded, biased, dogmatic, intolerant, fanatical, hateful, pessimistic, scientifically or politically biased, and so forth. Again, egotism can be an obstacle.

It becomes obvious when looking at this diagram that if a person has some of these attitudes, an open-minded approach would not be possible for this person. However, is there ever any awareness of how these attitudes have become habits through the years and have become submerged in the mind, resulting as obstacles with communication, learning, and development?

No doubt you have met some individuals and have tried to communicate with them only to realize how futile it can be to convey your thoughts and that it is fruitless to continue. I think that there is some old saying that a man convinced against his will is of the same opinion still. In many situations, decisions can be made quickly if it is not worthwhile to continue with discussions. It is certainly worthwhile to realize that it is better to avoid the frustrations of trying to communicate with or convince such a person.

Becoming open-minded is not an easy step, in a general sense, for anyone to take because of our upbringing, conditioning, and influences through our lives, as well as a variety of other factors. But if we are to learn and communicate, there needs to be some faith, understanding, and a willingness to listen with an open mind, without prejudice or bias, before making any judgement.

There can understandably be difficulties because of languages, and then there are the different terminologies with many of the sciences as well as various systems, disciplines, and modalities. Technology has advanced at a rapid rate during the last decade, with communication worldwide involving a large majority of the population.

With instant global communication, visual and audio transmission, language translations, various documentaries and commentaries on our television screens, we are presented with a much broader awareness of world affairs, but barriers of communication and understanding between different cultures, environments, and religious traditions, although closer, still remain.

Third illustration---a mind confined to rational thinking

Not listening and heeding one's thoughts to become creative and innovative

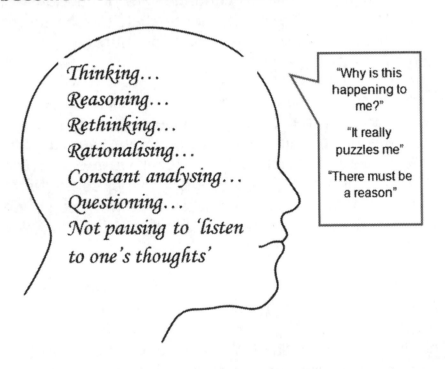

A positive and open-minded type of person, free of negative or restrictive attitudes, could be placed in this category. It could be someone who is interested in scientific studies, a person who is constantly thinking, reasoning, and asking questions but not pausing to listen to his or her thoughts, when often ideas and solutions come from the subconscious mind or higher levels of consciousness, to solve or to create.

Furthermore, an egotistical attitude hinders an open-minded approach. How much do we frequently restrict ourselves within the confines of rational thinking? How often do we find that an idea, a discovery, or a solution to a problem comes to us at a time when we are relaxed or engaged in some other activity yet we did not plan for this to happen? It happens to all of us. It is the mind solving the problem at a subconscious or higher level.

In his bath, Archimedes discovers the principle of specific gravity. Newton's resting under an apple tree and being hit on the head by a falling apple led to the laws of gravity and motion. And Einstein imagined that he was riding on a beam of light when making this statement: "Imagination is more important than knowledge."

Have you ever thought that it pays to think?

As a seventeen-year-old having passed a government public service examination, I was appointed to a position in the Education Department. It was my responsibility to organize and file the correspondence from schools in Victoria regarding school building maintenance repairs, new buildings, and so forth. In searching for files each day, it was necessary for me to check many of the offices in the building. Often I would need to check the director's office. He was rarely there because he was out visiting schools. How delightful it was for this young lad to spend a couple of minutes on most days sitting in his comfortable large swivel chair. It was my brief moments of relaxation and contemplation, wondering what the director of education would think about when he sat there.

The large desk was bare except for a small sign that read as follows: "Have you ever thought, it pays to think." It made me realize the importance that he placed on not becoming distracted and to remind himself to keep focused on thinking and contemplating. I know that those thoughts changed my approach to life in spending time in thinking and contemplation. Remember, all great discoveries, inventions, and many wonderful happenings began with just a thought or an idea.

"Allan, you were not listening to what was important to someone else."

Early in business life, we had a blinds, awnings, curtains, and drapes business. It was a cold winter's night and becoming dark at about six o'clock. As I was about to drive home for dinner, I saw a house with sheets hanging across the windows. What a pleasing sight it was to see a house with windows covered with bed sheets, obviously needing blinds, which provided me with an opportunity to leave a brochure with the homeowner. Although it was only my intention to make a friendly call to introduce myself and leave a brochure, the homeowner immediately invited me to come inside and measure for blinds.

So having collected my blind samples from the car, I proceeded to measure and write a quote, then giving a demonstration with a small venetian blind sample, explaining the quality of the product and its many benefits of light control, sunlight control, ventilation, privacy, the quality of the slatting and nylon cords, and so forth.

Then I paused when I sensed that the gentleman wanted to ask me a question. "Thank you, but what I would like to know is how soon can we get them installed? Here's a deposit." That was what was important to him. I made arrangements to fit the blinds at the end of the week. Driving back that evening, I remember laughing to myself and saying, "Allan, you weren't listening. What was important to that man was how soon he could get the blinds." With this came the realization of the importance of listening to the needs of customers and guiding them and assisting them in deciding what would best suit their needs. Life becomes much more worthwhile, enriching, and fulfilling when we listen and care for one another. We learn so much more about each other.

Years later as a chiropractor, there came the realization of how important it was to carefully listen to what a patient was telling me. By taking care to listen, the mind becomes more open to thoughts that come to guide us.

It is often easy to wake each day and switch on one's autopilot without having to think. What is it that we want to know? We need to first ask the questions and then be open-minded and wait for thoughts to come that will provide the answers to the knowledge that we seek.

Fourth illustration---Calmness of mind and being open-minded

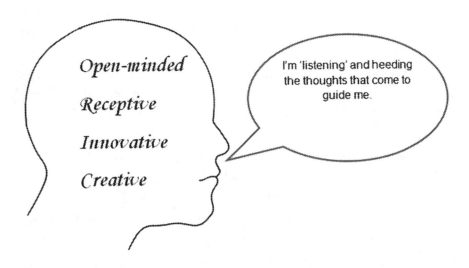

It is not easy for any of us to become open-minded. We each have our standards and principles of decent behaviour, but we can be open to new information or thoughts when studying the facts without prejudice before making decisions.

With decisions, actions and words in all aspects of life, I feel that Rotary International presents a worthwhile moral compass to guide with decisions, actions and words in respecting one another.

The Four Way Test of Rotary
Of the things we think, say or do.

IS IT THE TRUTH?
IS IT FAIR TO ALL CONCERNED?
WILL IT BUILD GOODWILL AND BETTER FRIENDSHIPS?
WILL IT BE BENEFICIAL TO ALL CONCERNED?

We should be open-minded—having the objective of being impartial, unbiased, or unprejudiced—with increasing awareness and understanding, developing positive thoughts and attitudes such as love, joy, friendship, caring, and enthusiasm. This will allow us to feel comfortable, confident, secure, and in control at all times as we enjoy life.

Being aware (communicating thoughts and producing feelings) stimulates our life force energy vortexes. Clear the mind of conscious thinking and then listen in order to hear and to heed thoughts, ideas, and solutions that often come from the subconscious mind or higher levels of consciousness. Furthermore, what is it that we want to know? We need to ask the questions and then listen to the thoughts that come in reply. Learning to listen was a major turning point in my life, to hear, to heed, and to guide me.

Chapter 11

Develop Your Vibrant New Self-Image, Enthusiastic, Energetic, Enjoying Life

The word enthusiasm is derived from the Greek *enthousiasmos*, from *enthous*—"possessed by a God." So let's get enthusiastic and release the divine, powerful God force within each of us. Enthusiasm radiates to everyone and releases that spontaneity of spirit, bringing with it those beautiful feelings of being energetic, excited, and exuberant, enjoying life and having fun. It's worthwhile to be enthusiastic!

Here are some suggestions to bring enthusiasm, energy, and enjoyment into routines that have become monotonous, boring, or tiring situations. Although it may seem to be only suitable for athletes and sports people, this type of approach can be applied to any situation.

Let's suppose, for example, that the coach tells you to do eight 150-metre runs at three quarter pace, with only a brief recovery period in between each run. If these runs have become a routine part of your training schedule, it can often happen, with the lack of variety and the monotony of routine, that boredom or staleness can sometimes creep in. You don't enjoy training as much as previously, and it becomes easy to slide into the doldrums. Perhaps this is one of the reasons that there is sometimes a breakdown in the relationships between athletes, and their coaches.

With our guided relaxation session, the art of instant relaxation was to focus on the breathing and perceive the air as it came automatically in and out of the nostrils. Immediately your mind becomes totally absorbed in perceiving your breathing automatically and feeling all that is happening in your body.

Now let's get back to the track with your focus and feeling on how you are running so that you can enjoy these 150-metre runs.

Are you aware that it will produce beneficial results if you do these 150-metre runs in your imagination? And are you aware that mental training is an important part of any training, as explained in the next chapter. You are most welcome to join with me in these runs, in our imaginations.

First run: Remember the relaxed, rhythmical arm swinging, with focus on the wrists.

Second run: Focus on long striding and feel yourself floating over the ground.

Third run: Relax and focus on high knee lifting with relaxed arm-swinging movements.

Fourth run: Imagine running on hot coals. Run with a fast and light pitter-patter action.

Fifth run:	Feel coordination between whole arm movements, shoulders, wrists, and ankles.
Sixth run:	Run relaxed with long strides and lift the knees high as you float over the ground.
Seventh run:	Smile. Feel enthusiastic, energetic, and excited as you enjoy running down the track.
Eighth run:	You are now "poetry in motion." Give an exhibition run. Listen to the applause.

After each run, let your breathing recover in whatever way feels comfortable for you. Before and after each of the runs, do three, four, or more Vortex Energy breathing techniques. I would suggest the technique of lifting the shoulders and rolling the shoulders backwards, with your focus on the upper chest as you push your elbows backwards, forcing the upper lung space to expand, causing the air to flow in effortlessly.

You are now activating the neural pathways for all these movements, but more than that, you are also mentally as well as physically training your body with enthusiasm, energy, and enjoyment, making it exciting. Mental training is equally as important as physical training, as the nervous system does not distinguish between your physical training and what you perform in your imagination.

Let's assume you are running eight 400-metre runs.

First run:	Start slowly and gradually increase to a three-quarter pace towards the finish.
Second run:	Commence slowly and gradually increase your speed to a three-quarter pace into mid section and slow down gradually.

Third run:	Have an even pace throughout, focusing on enjoyment and being relaxed.
Fourth run:	At the start, gradually work up to three-quarter pace and stride as far as possible.
Fifth run:	Use your sprint start, relaxed sprinting style and take long strides.
Sixth run:	Use a relaxed, varied sprinting style.
Seventh run:	Relaxed sprint start and then change to long striding. Then relax sprint.
Eighth run:	Become enthusiastic and enjoy a relaxed three-quarter pace even run.

Here is a valuable point to remember at the finish of each 400-metre run. Do not stop suddenly but use the momentum that you already have to carry yourself as far as you can, just striding relaxed, so that you are actually running more than the 400 metres. This is to develop extra stamina, and it also reduces the risk of injury. It is also training your body to hold good running form, particularly at the end of races.

Warming up slowly is important in order to avoid injuries and perform better.

It is most important to warm up slowly before commencing training, even with distance runners. It is a worthwhile approach in avoiding injuries as well as performing better. For any athlete or sports person, two or three laps at a slow flat-footed shuffle in a warm tracksuit is recommended. A gradual smooth increase in pace or speed minimizes the risk of injuries and improves performances. This is only intended as a brief outline of a warm-up routine; more can be added, such as making a series of wind sprints part of the routine.

Wind sprints

Wind sprints are invaluable for maintaining your speed as well as developing stamina. Just visualizing the running track, you can either walk or jog slowly around the curves. Then do the wind sprints down each side of the track. Commence each wind sprint by gradually increasing your pace to half-pace over the first 25 metres. Continue at a half pace for 25 metres and then gradually let your body slow down for 25 metres. After perhaps eight or ten wind sprints, depending on your training schedule, then you could increase your speed to three-quarter or almost top speed for the remaining wind sprints, whatever number suits your overall training routine, which can of course vary each day.

With this approach, there is no sudden acceleration from the start. Gradually accelerating to almost top pace allows the athlete to run and develop an easy, relaxed, balanced, and coordinated running style.

Wind sprints, apart from developing stamina and being an excellent form of training to improve speed, are also worthwhile in ensuring that speed is gradually increased, therein helping to avoid injuries by any sudden exertion.

Self-image: a most common factor adversely affecting performances

Again, the self-image is a subconscious perception that one has of one's appearance, capabilities, and personality. Of course, this can also be a conscious perception that a person can have. The development of the self-image commences during our early formative years as a result of the many influences from parents, teachers, peer groups, and all that is seen and heard. It sets imaginary boundaries, parameters, or limitations on one's capabilities. It will retard or hinder an individual from performing beyond the restricting limitations of this self-image, even though consciously there is a strong desire to achieve some particular goals.

It is fascinating when testing to find that the mind-brain-body records the memory of the age when stress adversely affected the child during the early formative years.

From my experiences as a result of testing, it would seem that a negative self-image generally commences about the age of five years as a result of experiencing some stressful situations. I believe that it happens around this time because that's usually the period when a child starts school. It is easy to think of many new situations and surroundings as well as missing one's parents making it stressful for most children to attend school for the first time. This is only suggested as one factor.

With testing, it can be demonstrated that a negative self-image is similar to a stress pattern in that it is submerged in the mind at a subconscious level. It can also be demonstrated if and how the self-image affects the neurological and musculoskeletal aspects of mind-body function. With testing, it becomes evident that all the vortexes test weak, which would suggest that all of the body's main innate feelings have been affected as a result of stress.

A self-image that has been negatively affected is a most common phenomenon.

It is similar to a stress pattern in that it is submerged in the mind at a subconscious level. The adverse effects can be demonstrated by the practitioner saying the words "your self-image" while using an indicator testing muscle of the person to obtain this information. But the self-image affects the body differently from a stress pattern. The practitioner will find that that weakness is evident when his or her hand is held about three inches above each vortex. It has been found that the reason for this is that the body's innate feelings have been affected—that is, love, comfort, security, sensual pleasure, control, and expression.

Our Vortex Energy Therapy presentations and demonstrations provide an opportunity to teach and to have the person demonstrate the immediate effectiveness of the self-help breathing technique in making the correction and restoring a new self-image.

How can a happy, friendly, kind, caring, vibrant, confident, and radiant new self-image be developed? Every time you have your revitalizing, relaxation session, when you are experiencing that beautiful state of being, the alpha state, see yourself at that moment as being the person that you would like to be. Remember the guided relaxation, personal development, and goal-setting visualization sessions in chapter 8. When you set your goals of what you would like to achieve while you are in this most pleasant, relaxed state of being, your wonderful mind-brain-body biological computer will guide you in the direction to achieve your goals.

How can a confident, vibrant new self-image remain part of one's life?

Even though one might be feeling on top of the world, it is only natural that there can be doubts, frustration, anxiety, fears, and so forth. A person can be feeling really well, but then doubts or feelings of anxiety might creep into one's thinking. In our presentation and demonstration sessions, the person who is being tested is shown these words written on a piece of paper. It becomes obvious with testing that looking at these words has weakened the person and adversely affected the new self-image.

It is then explained that these words registered in the conscious mind, which immediately relayed these discordant negative words to the subconscious mind, producing an overall adverse effect on the body, this marvellous biological computer that records all instructions from the conscious mind. How can this be corrected? What is the most beautiful and powerful feeling in the universe? Yes, it is love! Gradually it can be recognized that anytime there are doubts, anxiety, frustration, fears, and so forth, just thinking "with love and gratitude" will immediately recharge your body overall, with energy that is also radiating out from your body. Every time you have a glass of water, think, *With love and gratitude.*

After using the corrective VET techniques, the beneficial results immediately become evident. It can be then replaced with a vibrant, wholesome new self-image. It is most important for our younger generation, especially during the difficult period through the teenage years. Although this book is suitable for everyone, the teenage years would be the most important time for all of us to focus on and to help our younger generation.

> *The "self-image" is the key to human personality and human behaviour. Change the self-image and you change the personality and the behaviour. But more than this. The "self-image" sets the boundaries of individual accomplishment. It defines what you can and cannot do. Expand the self-image and you expand the "area of the possible." The development of an adequate, realistic self-image will seem to imbue the individual with new capabilities, new talents and literally turn failure into success.*
>
> —**Maxwell Maltz, MD, FICS**
> *Psycho-Cybernetics*

Chapter 12

Facilitating Learning and Developing New Skills

The aim of this program is to arrive at the stage of performing the movements automatically, with little conscious thought. Playing the piano is an example, reading the music and playing automatically, as a result training the fingers through many years of practice with each phrase of the music without much conscious thought about which keys the fingers should touch. And with ballroom dancing, you move harmoniously with your partner while performing many intricate steps and movements as you both glide together as one around the floor, in time with the rhythm of the music, feeling those wonderful moments. Do I sound like an old romantic? Well, I am!

How VET facilitates the learning and development of new skills:

First	An overall assessment is made to determine a person's physical condition.
Second	Vortex Energy Therapy techniques are used to bring mind-brain-body function to its potential.

Third	Become aware of what is not known about the new skills by observing with guided commentary the actual performances you would like to emulate—for example, watching videos, DVDs, and so forth, to mentally imprint a variety of movement sequence patterns.
Fourth	Practise each movement. This phase is combined with Vortex Energy techniques to activate the neural pathways within for each movement sequence pattern. The VET self-help breathing techniques are immediately effective. This movement sequence pattern technique, which results in all muscles functioning in synchronization, takes into consideration the muscles of posture combined with the body in motion. It also activates and forms new neural pathways for each new skill.

Continue to practise until you begin to feel comfortable with the movement, and then you do not consciously think about the movements but focus on what you want to achieve. This is an important step, not always easy because of the habit of thinking so much previously about the movements and so forth.

With touch typing, for example, there will be the tendency to be thinking about the location of the keys on the computer and which fingers should be used with each key. Of course, it is most likely there will be mistakes at first, but with persistence it will gradually be found that the movement becomes automatic, without as much conscious thought that was needed previously with practising.

How does the VET approach facilitate the learning of new skills?

It is the use of the techniques to initially correct and eliminate many detrimental factors and faulty habits that have developed during the formative years, such as stress patterns, posture, gait, coordination, and so on, as discussed in chapter 1. This has always been routine procedure when testing, assessing, and using the VET techniques to make corrections with anyone for the first time. The objective of the whole program is to bring mind-brain-body function to its highest level of efficiency. These aims involve checking and correcting all levels of the body to ensure that the whole body is balanced, with all systems functioning in synchronization and movements all coordinated.

Remember the old adage that practice makes perfect? But beware of practising faulty habits. Competent coaching and guidance are most important. It has often been found with testing during our VET program that many imbalances have resulted from the exercises that the athlete or football player has been doing, sometimes with the guidance of coaches. The VET arm-swinging method is of paramount importance in correcting the overall imbalances with movement.

Please understand and be assured that these comments are not intended as a criticism of anyone, for it has only been from my being in the position to be able to later check and test in making these discoveries. Here is an example of how discoveries can eventuate. One patient who had responded very well with treatment suddenly developed knee pain. What was the cause? What had he been doing that was different? He had commenced training with a personal trainer who had given him the exercise of vigorously swinging his arms while standing in the one spot.

Testing revealed that the cause of the knee pain was that this vigorous, tense arm swinging was throwing the body completely out of balance and causing knee pain. This test made me realize the importance of our VET arm-swinging exercises to correct and restore the overall balance of the body and coordination with movement.

Visualization and mentally imprinting the movement sequence pattern

There are many approaches for mentally imprinting movement sequences with learning new skills at a subconscious mind level. There are many examples, such as hitting a golf ball down the fairway. The main thought the golfer has is where he or she intends the ball to land. Any necessary calculations with visualization are made before the golf swing. So many factors, such as weather conditions, need to be taken into consideration with golf. Golfers have reached a high level of precision in visualizing their goal of seeing the ball go into the hole. Learning new skills is similar in all sports—tennis, athletics, running, football, soccer, basketball, and so on.

Learning to perform and perfect any types of skills might require the relevant guidance and many hours, months, or years of practice, but the Vortex Energy techniques facilitate and enhance the entire learning process, with the correction and elimination of muscular imbalances within a wide variety of movements. These corrections are made before commencing any practice.

Often in absorbing new skills, a player can become focused and overburdened by too many instructions to consciously carry out. Furthermore, in most cases, with posture, balance, and so on, it is often difficult for anyone to adapt from what seems to be a comfortable posture or movement. These adaptive changes can be corrected to enhance posture, balance, coordination, and overall mind-body function before teaching new skills.

In a nutshell

The VET techniques facilitate the learning of new skills by first bringing the mind-brain-body function to its highest level of efficiency, becoming aware of the new skills by watching your coach or DVDs with guidance to imprint the complete movements subconsciously in your mind; activating the neural pathways specifically for the movements of the skills that you would like to emulate; and becoming enthusiastic while enjoying practising, practising, practising.

Fast and slow tempos—walking and running with changes of pace

Furthermore, this neurological dysfunction becomes evident with testing, when adapting to different tempos of the music. This is also evident with testing after using a metronome. The same techniques will correct this particular aspect, which is most important. Also, as explained in chapter 2, there is a simple technique to make corrections to enable the body to adapt to a change of pace or tempo without any overall weakening effect.

Chapter 13

Rebalancing the Body after Injury

As explained at the beginning of our program, when testing anyone for the first time, the body is predisposed to injuries because of many common detrimental factors, overall imbalances, and faulty habits. VET techniques correct and eliminate all these adverse factors. But it is as equally important to ensure that the body is balanced after recovering from injury. The VET techniques immediately make these corrections in restoring and rebalancing the body after injury.

Using strained or torn hamstrings and knee injuries as examples

From my experience with treating strained or torn hamstrings, here are the reasons that this is such a common and frequently recurring injury. For the benefit of everyone, it would be worthwhile to briefly explain about these muscles. The three muscles located at the back (posterior) of the thigh are most commonly known as the hamstrings, the biceps femoris muscle (lateral hamstring) and the semitendinosus and semimembranosus muscles (medial hamstrings).

The opposite group of muscles on the front of the thigh are known as the quadriceps and consist of the rectus femoris muscle, the vastus medialis muscle, the vastus intermedius muscle, and the vastus lateralis muscle.

For example, quadriceps (the agonist muscles) contract and hamstrings (the antagonist muscles) relax, but when the hamstrings contract immediately after the quadriceps relax, these hamstring muscles cannot contract strongly because there is a dysfunctional neurological mechanism in which there is a three to four second delay because of inhibitory neurological impulses acting on the hamstrings, preventing these muscles from contracting at full strength, predisposing the hamstrings to being strained or even torn.

Knee injuries

There is a similar situation that can occur at the knee joint because of two muscles involved: the sartorius, which is the longest muscle in the body, spanning two joints, the hip and the knee; and then there is the popliteus muscle at the back of the knee, which stabilizes the knee joint. In this case, the delay in the timing mechanism with the neurological inhibitory impulses acting on the popliteus results in instability at the knee joint, causing it to collapse or become predisposed to injury at some stage.

Impairment of the sacral and coccygeal nerves, as explained in chapter 4, "The Mind-Brain-Body Biological Computer"

Many of the muscles at the back of the leg are innervated by nerves from the fourth and fifth lumbar nerve routes and especially the first and second sacral nerves. The gluteal muscles, hamstrings, popliteus, gastrocnemius, and soleus muscles are all involved. Correcting and eliminating this impairment to the sacral nerves is again a major contributing factor with treatment. The elimination of this impairment of sacral nerve function immediately produces an overall improvement in correcting any adverse effects with body function. There may also need to be corrections made if there are adhesions preventing movement of the coccyx bone, as this could be causing tension on the spinal cord.

The objective of the Vortex Energy Therapy program is to prevent injuries and to remove the cause by bringing mind-brain body function to its highest level of efficiency and eliminating the factors that are predisposing the body to injuries and serving as a hindrance to performing at one's potential. All aspects of the program are important in order to achieve these objectives. It can be demonstrated in one session how the Vortex Energy Therapy techniques quickly achieve these objectives. Treatment of injuries are not a part of the Vortex Energy Therapy program but can be used by qualified practitioners to do so.

If there is a tear in the fibres of the muscle, the actin and myosin fibres need time to heal, with appropriate treatment by the practitioner. After healing has occurred, scar tissue is formed at the site of the lesion and the muscle fibres can usually be felt bunched together in this region. This can be felt by rolling the tips of the fingers transversely across the muscle. Deep transverse massage with the finger tips by the practitioner has been found to be effective in removing the scar tissue, as it results in rolling the actin and myosin fibrils apart in diminishing the scar. If the scar tissue is not removed, the muscle is predisposed to a recurring injury because with contraction of the muscle, the actin and myosin fibrils cannot slide into each other because of the scar tissue preventing this from happening. This is one of the factors predisposing the muscles to recurring injuries. There is also a Vortex Energy Therapy technique to restore blockages in energy flow caused by scar tissue.

With most sporting injuries, overall muscular imbalances result because of the body adjusting and adapting to rebalance, usually to relieve pain or reduce pressure on the injury. When the injury heals, these adaptive imbalances remain. It is most important to restore the overall balance, coordination, and synchronization of muscle function with movement. Otherwise, the body remains predisposed to recurring injuries.

Athletes are always anxious to quickly recover from injuries and resume training because of concern to maintain their level of fitness. From my point of view, it has always been important to ensure that the athlete is completely fit to commence training without any remaining predisposing factors likely to cause injuries. In order to achieve this level of fitness with body function, much care has been taken to balance the whole musculature of the body with coordination and synchronization of muscle function with movement. With any injuries, the body will adapt and compensate to a comfortable position to take strain and pressure off the injury.

My good friends Anne and Ron Stobaus presented me with this amazing story about Anne's outstanding performances in winning gold medals and breaking world records after recovering from strained hamstrings. It seems to be appropriate in following on with this story as a case study. I am thankful to Anne and Ron for providing these details.

Anne came to our home limping with strained muscles, unable to train because of pain and restriction with movement. She did have expectations of competing in the 2011 World Masters Games in California, which were due to commence in less than four weeks. How amazing to have such a level of fitness to be competing as a seventy-year-old old in so many world-class events over a wide range of distances, 100, 200, 400 and 800 metres. She had been particularly looking forward to competing at these games because for the first time in her running career, she would be competing in the same age category as Jeane D'Aprano the superstar of World Masters Athletics, undefeated over 400, 800 and 1500 metres throughout her running career. What a grand achievement also for Jeane D'Aprano to be able to maintain fitness in competing and performing at such an elite level. It certainly proves that her training routines have been well worthwhile

Anne began her running career when she turned fifty, with the aim of improving her speed when playing tennis, a sport she had enjoyed for many years. How fortunate it was for Anne to have the guidance of her husband, Ron, head coach of Keilor St Bernard's Athletic Club. It certainly turned out to become a successful winning partnership, for during the next twenty-two years, Anne won twenty-one World medals and seventy National medals and also competed in inter-club competition with her daughters and granddaughters.

Through the years, Ron has been devoted, with outstanding success, to coaching athletes. He has received many accolades and been the recipient of many awards for the champions and winning teams that he has coached. Testament to his many outstanding accomplishments and his dedication with coaching and guiding athletes has been the acknowledgement of his peers with his induction into St Bernard's College hallowed Hall of Fame, a fitting tribute to a great coach.

But let's continue with our story about assisting Anne to overcome her problem with being unable to train because of the pain and restriction of movement. Without going into detail, our approach was to not focus only on the strained muscles but to make overall corrections with balance and coordination. The most important phase with correction was to teach the VET arm-swinging exercises to ensure overall balance and coordination with sprinting; otherwise, the possibility of a recurrence would have been most likely. It was pleasing to see the immediate overall response at the end of this session, with Anne testing well. Anne came again the following week so that we could make further corrections, which we found were not needed. Our focus was then on using techniques for relaxation and suppleness of the muscles.

In resuming training after injury, depending on the situation and assuming the athlete is capable of training, wind sprints, as described in chapter 11, would be a worthwhile approach to quickly regain fitness and stamina and maintain speed. It is most important to warm up slowly before commencing training, even with distance runners.

2011 World Masters Games, California (excerpts from report by Ron Stobaus)

Jeane D'Aprano and Anne competed against each other in the 200, 400 and 800 metres for the first time. The 800 metres was a great tussle with Jeane winning by ½ second. Both ran amazing times with Anne breaking the Australian record. Their next event, the 200 metres, saw Anne finishing 3rd and Jeane 4th.

The day of the 400 metres dawned and we headed early to the track for Anne to prepare. Anne started at her usual fast pace and by the 200 metre mark had overtaken most of the field including Jeane, who was in hot pursuit as they powered up the track to the finish line. Anne crossed the line, her name appearing on the board with a time of 76.33 seconds, a World Record—mission accomplished!

How exciting it was to hear of Anne's great performances in California. She won three gold medals, one silver medal, and one bronze medal. In doing this, she broke the 400 metres world record.

Then the Australian relay team, with Anne Lang, Noreen Parrish, Anne Stobaus, and Peggy Macliver won gold medals and broke a world record in winning the 4 x 400 metres, with more gold medals coming for the team in winning the 4 x 100 metres.

What a wonderful achievement by the whole team. How superbly fit and conditioned they would be to be able to compete in so many races at such a high level as the World Masters Games. It certainly proves their training routines and preparation.

Photos: Christina Bortignon, Canada; Anne Stobaus, Australia; Jeane D'Aprano, USA

Anne Stobaus, Ron Stobaus (coach), Jeane D'Aprano

The 2011 World Masters Games, California, USA: Anne Lang, Noreen Parrish, Anne Stobaus, Peggy MacLiver (left to right)

Photos courtesy of Ron Stobaus

Chapter 14

Exciting Features of Vortex Energy Therapy

An Overview and Recap of Exciting Discoveries and Features

An outstanding feature of the VET program is that in one session of approximately an hour, self-help breathing, movement, and arm-swinging techniques to correct and eliminate many common detrimental factors can be explained and demonstrated. The marked improvement immediately becomes evident after the use of each technique. The program focuses on teaching these techniques as well as self-help relaxation, revitalization, and goal-setting visualization techniques. It is a program suitable and beneficial for everyone.

With the development of the program, it was of paramount importance to ensure that the techniques fulfilled the criteria as being scientifically valid so that with each technique, the results could be precisely predicted, the overall improvements could be measured in different ways, and these results could be repeated by anyone. As the program has been developed in a gradual step-by-step procedure on a solid structural foundation, it has not been difficult to satisfy the criteria of predictability, measurability, and repeatability, because each proven discovery has served as a step and led to further discoveries. With each discovery, there has been a definite purpose in searching for solutions to help patients with a variety of injuries and ailments.

You can be assured with all of the claims made about the immediate beneficial effects resulting from the use of each technique that there is not any exaggeration. Every technique can be confirmed, explained, and shown via demonstrations. It is much more than hypothesizing or theorizing. It is complementary and blends with other forms of treatment

The formative years

Muscular imbalances, structural misalignments, and faulty habits commence to develop in the early formative years, especially during that period from crawling to the upright posture and walking, with the learning of a wide variety of movement sequences and new skills, the formation of one's self-image, the physical maturing through the period of puberty, finding one's direction and goals during the difficult teenage years, with gradual physical maturing to adulthood.

Common detrimental factors

When initially testing anyone, it is expected to find many common detrimental factors present. You may remember these factors from chapter 1—stress patterns; impairment of the sacral and coccygeal nerves; extreme changes in weather temperature; airborne pollutants; and negative attitudes, thoughts, feelings, emotions, and so forth.

It is understandable that there does not seem to be much awareness of these common detrimental factors, because it has only been after years of research and testing that awareness of the adverse effects of these factors has developed to become part of the whole Vortex Energy Therapy program.

If these faulty habits from the formative years and common detrimental factors are not corrected and eliminated, the body remains predisposed to injuries and illnesses and is not capable of functioning with maximal efficiency. With all injuries and ailments, it is of paramount importance to remove the cause in order to prevent recurrences. The VET techniques correct and eliminate the cause.

To understand the Vortex Energy Therapy program it is worthwhile to remember the purpose, aim, and principle of the whole program in focusing on the self-help techniques, which are not time-consuming but can be embraced into your everyday routine activities, with each technique taking just a few seconds. You can take three or four breaths while sitting at your desk or the table, do relaxed, rhythmical arm-swinging exercises for a minute or less, close your eyes while sitting in a chair or resting on the bed, and relax completely and perceive your breathing happening automatically. Always be sure to keep warm during any relaxing sessions and make yourself comfortable when resting.

Affirmations and Our Innate Feelings

Consider again our affirmation verse:

> *With feelings of love, kindness, caring, and gratitude,*
> *I am enriching my life by improving my attitude.*
> *I am breathing in the energy to ensure*
> *I feel calm, comfortable, confident, secure,*
> *In control at all times, in every situation,*
> *Revitalizing with breathing and relaxation.*

As mentioned in chapter 1, affirmations become much more powerful when the innate feelings, important for body function, are included in the affirmations and produce immediate and overall beneficial effects in the body.

Each line of the verse could be in your mind as thoughts rhythmically blending with each breath. As I breathe in, I think of the line or a phrase and then completely relax when breathing out, just focusing on taking a fresh breath with every line. Perhaps there may be one or two lines that appeal to you more than the others. If so, make those lines your main affirmations. You do whatever you feel suits you best.

And of course you remember the rest of the affirmation verse:

> *Enthusiastic, energetic, enjoying life, having fun,*
> *with dear friends I care for, each and every one.*
> *I am enriching my life by improving my attitude,*
> *With feelings of love, kindness, caring, and gratitude.*

The mind-brain-body functions as a marvellous biological computer. Chapter 4, "The Mind-Brain-Body Biological Computer," explains how to access and correct numerous dysfunctional neurological circuits at this level or frequency.

The whole body can be thought of as a touch computer screen. On its surface, there are many points through which information can be accessed by touching a point while at the same time testing if a strong indicator testing muscle tests weak or strong. Weakness indicates that there is a break in life force energy flow in a circuitry. Each body point provides us with information about the body's condition.

A multidimensional circuitry functioning at many levels or frequencies

Information can be quickly accessed from all levels of the body. It is easy to interchange from one level to another to diagnose the cause of the ailment.

Impairment of function of the sacral and coccygeal nerves

As discussed in chapter 4, "The Mind-Brain-Body Biological Computer," it has been a most important discovery and an outstanding feature of the program to discover that everyone tested had impairment of function with the sacral and coccygeal nerves. It can be readily appreciated the multitude of ailments that can occur within the pelvis because of impaired neural function in this region.

Breathing in harmony and synchronisation with all bodily systems

It is recommended that the self-help breathing techniques are used regularly to expand and increase capacity; to breathe in a relaxed, automatic, rhythmical manner; to restore energy; and to make overall corrections.

With VET techniques, you are relaxed and not trying to breathe but just letting the breathing happen automatically in response to the body's overall energy requirements

The two main breathing techniques are the arching of the lower back as you breathe in and the lifting and rolling back of the shoulders. Refer to Chapter 5, "Balance and Revitalize Your Body."

Posture balancing and coordinated movement sequences

Most people change their postures through their lives to adapt to circumstances, work, injuries, and habits. In making corrections, VET techniques facilitate and activate the neural pathways for a relaxed, balanced, and erect posture, with the centre of gravity line running through the weight-bearing joints of the spine and parallel to the femur and tibia bones to the ankle joints.

The body's overall balance needs to be checked while standing, sitting, running and moving to acquire a relaxed, and balance posture.

Arm-swinging technique

The arm-swinging exercise coordinates and synchronizes the joints of the arms and legs, particularly to ensure that the wrists and ankles are functioning in synchronization at the same rates.

To experience the feeling of relaxation, bend both arms at right angles at the elbows. Let your arms drop completely relaxed and swing effortlessly for two or three seconds and then follow up with the arm-swinging exercises. Become conscious of the whole arm movement, from the shoulder joints to the wrists and hands.

Now start walking, letting the arms hang completely relaxed and swing rhythmically in tempo with the pace that you have set. As you increase your pace, you will feel the overall balance and coordination, and then you can consciously swing your arms faster. Your arms will also swing faster in synchronization with the faster pace.

With sprinting or running at a fast pace, the postural balance or forward body lean can be determined by the level or height of the hands at the end of the arc with each arm swing.

It's always beneficial to practise your arm-swinging at any time to feel the overall balance and coordination in your body. A minute or less is well worthwhile.

Relaxation, revitalization, and goal-setting visualization

Chapter 8, "A Guided Relaxation, Personal Development, Goal-Setting Visualization Session," presents suggestions to help with relaxation in perceiving your breath as you inhale and exhale through your nostrils and feel the automatic functioning of your body. It is the art of immediately relaxing.

When you are in a beautiful state of relaxation, you visualize yourself at that moment doing and achieving whatever you would like to happen. These powerful thoughts will guide you to accomplish these goals. This is the time to develop a new vibrant self-image.

Touching with healing hands expressing feelings of kindness, comfort, and love

We communicate our feelings with touch. Touch is the language of the universe. Touch is a language all of its own. Without words, we communicate our thoughts, feelings and emotions. A mother touches and nurtures her baby with love and joy. We embrace to silently comfort one another and share our feelings of love in times of sadness.

Kindness, caring concern, and compassion

Every day around the world, many kind, caring, concerned, and compassionate people give generously of themselves in helping others who are in need. Many are members of large organizations; others are part of the community. It is most unlikely that we know or will ever hear of such people, for they give unobtrusively of themselves in helping others.

In many places around the world, thousands of people have suddenly found themselves homeless, without food, shelter, and warmth, caused by the devastation of natural disasters such as fire, floods, tsunamis, cyclones, earthquakes, and blizzards. Then there are the issues of famine, disease, lack of clean drinking water and sanitation, pain and suffering from chronic conditions, and, sadly, traumas from inhumane atrocities.

Love, caring, kindness, and compassion are our natural innate feelings that we have within us as human beings in reaching out to help others. We reach out with spontaneity of spirit to embrace, to touch, to comfort, and to help in whatever way we can.

Each one of us is unique. We each have a purpose in life. We may not always be aware of what that purpose might be, but if we pause and listen, providence will guide each of us along the path that has been chosen for us to follow— to learn, to love, respect, and serve one another; to smile, laugh, and have fun; and enjoy ourselves along the way.

Thank you. Valerie would be very happy that at last we have been able to share this information with you.

This book would not be complete until I express my heartfelt thanks to my dear Valerie for all her help and encouragement. In the earliest days of our courtship, this photo was taken at our first dancing date. It was the beginning of our wonderful lifetime together. It was with Val's encouragement that I studied chiropractic as a mature age student because she felt it was my "niche in life". Valerie's assistance, support, and contributions in so many ways gradually resulted in the development of our Vortex Energy Therapy system and now, thanks be to God, this joyful moment of publishing our first book, *Peak Performance, Enjoyment and Well-Being.*

Knowledge from around the World

Books relevant to the Vortex Energy Therapy program

From China – the meridian system, which is the basis of traditional Chinese medicine and is utilized in the practice of acupuncture

From India – the practice of yoga: the chakras, subtle bodies, breathing, and relaxation

From Japan – the research of Dr Hiroshi Motoyama: *Science and the Evolution of Consciousness, Chakras, Ki, and Psi* as well as many other books.

From Thailand – the Healing Tao System, developed by Mantak Chia.

Vibrational Medicine, by Richard Gerber, MD

Joy's Way, by W. Brugh Joy, MD

Science of the Gods, by David Ash and Peter Hewitt

The Tao of Physics, The Turning Point, The Web of Life, and *The Science of Leonardo*, by Dr Fritjof Capra

Encounters with Einstein and Other Essays on People, Places, and Particles, by Werner Heisenberg

Psycho-Cybernetics, by Maxwell Maltz, MD, FICS

The Healing Power of Water as well as other books by Masaru Emoto

Living Water: Viktor Schauberger and the Secrets of Natural Energy, by Olof Alexandersson

Heal Your Body, by Louise L. Hay

You Can Heal Your Life, by Louise L. Hay

The Essential Wayne W. Dyer Collection—The Power of Intention, The Shift, and *Excuses Begone*—as well as *Wisdom of the Ages* and many other books by Wayne Dyer

Ageless Body, Timeless Mind; *Grow Younger, Live Longer*; and many other books by Deepak Chopra

Books by Tom Butler-Bowdon: *50 Self-Help Classics, 50 Success Classics, 50 Spiritual Classics, 50 Psychology Classics, 50 Prosperity Classics, 50 Philosophy Classics, Never Too Late to Be Great*

Printed in the United States
By Bookmasters